Walter Cranston Larned

Churches and Castles of Mediæval France

Walter Cranston Larned

Churches and Castles of Mediæval France

ISBN/EAN: 9783744791793

Printed in Europe, USA, Canada, Australia, Japan

Cover: Foto ©ninafisch / pixelio.de

More available books at **www.hansebooks.com**

CHURCHES AND CASTLES OF MEDIÆVAL FRANCE

BY

WALTER CRANSTON LARNED

ILLUSTRATED

NEW YORK
CHARLES SCRIBNER'S SONS
1895

To my daughter Elsie
in loving memory of her dear companionship
in these journeyings

_*[*]_* THIS book is a record of a traveller's impressions of the great monuments of France. I hope that it may bring others to see these wonderful churches and castles. It is easy for the student to get accurate information about them; but nevertheless it may be of some use to tell what effect they produce upon one who does not wish to study deeply into all their history and the minute details of the building of them, but who does love their beauty and cares about the place they hold in the history of the French people.

W. C. L.

CONTENTS

vii

ILLUSTRATIONS

CHURCHES AND CASTLES OF MEDIÆVAL FRANCE

CHURCHES AND CASTLES OF
MEDIÆVAL FRANCE

CHAPTER I

HISTORICAL MONUMENTS OF FRANCE

No one who has travelled in France, and visited
the cathedrals, the châteaux, and the walled towns,
can fail to be deeply impressed by the meaning of
the two words, "historical monument." These words
are found in every guide-book. Sometimes only the
initials (M. H.) are given, as in Murray. A "monument historique" in France means a church, or a
castle, or a town that has been thought worthy either
of restoration or preservation at the expense of the
French people. There is a tax levied to provide the
money nècessary for these purposes, and it is astonishing how much the French are willing to pay to
preserve or restore whatever has to do with their
history as a nation. The money required is by no
means a small sum. The restoration of Carcassonne
was undertaken by Mr. Viollet-le-Duc, by the direc-

tion of the authorities who have these matters in charge in France. This restoration meant spending about four hundred thousand dollars on the cathedral and about three hundred thousand dollars on the walls and towers. The work is not yet completed. The château, which was an important part of the old town, is not yet completely restored, and it will cost a large sum of money before that is finished, in the same way as the cathedral and the walls and towers have been now made nearly as they were when they were built.

The same thing has been done at Nîmes, though not at so great a cost. But this is only one among many illustrations as to the spirit of the French people in this matter. The Château of Pierrefonds was also restored by Mr. Viollet-le-Duc in the time of Louis Napoleon. It attests again his skill in bringing mediæval buildings, apparently dead, back again to the life that was theirs at the time when they were built.

The outlay of money does not cease even when the restorations are completed. There must be a "custodian" for every historical monument, and he must have a house to live in and a salary to support him. Of course the fees given by visitors are no small part of his remuneration, but, nevertheless, he is a government official, and the government is responsible for his maintenance.

There are many places in France where other questions as to money are involved in the preservation of the ancient monuments. Bayonne is an example in point. This was a very strongly fortified town in the Middle Ages. The walls of the town are mostly preserved. The moat is there, too, although not now full of water. The fortified gates, the ramparts, still are there, and the bastions and barbicans outside the walls. All these take up an immense amount of space, and every foot of land they cover would be valuable for business purposes, because Bayonne is a flourishing city, — a seaport, growing every day in commercial importance. Nevertheless, the old walls and moat, the barbicans and bastions, are not disturbed. They are kept as monuments to the glory of France, and also for illustration of history. They must inspire the French with patriotic devotion to their own land.

There is a lesson to be learned here as to the enlightenment of the French people at the present day, and there is another lesson to be learned, by way of contrast, in going back to the French Revolution, and seeing that no social convulsion the world has ever seen destroyed so many relics of the past as did that one. Not even the iconoclasts of Cromwell were so unsparing in wanton destruction. It seems as if the French of to-day were trying to make amends for the fearful excesses of those who were goaded to madness by the tyranny of king after king, culminating in the frightful contrast between the luxury of Louis XIV.'s court and the misery of his people.

The fury past, calmness regained, free government assured, the people value as precious things all that remains in visible form to tell of their ancient history.

It is not only those connected with the government who feel in this way. The common people are in full sympathy with this feeling. The custodian of Carcassonne said, with pride, that he paid his share of the tax for the restoration of the ancient place like any other citizen, although he is a government official; and the same thing would be said by all those who take care of the French historical monuments.

This custodian of Carcassonne is a remarkable man. He has the courtesy of a gentleman, the knowledge of a scholar about his own subject, and much intelligence about other matters beside.

The custodian of Aigues-Mortes is equally courteous and equally intelligent. The guide-books cannot tell what these men know. They have made the one thing that is entrusted to their care the sole study of their lives. They love it and they know it.

It would be well if the American people would take care of such historical monuments as they have in the same way as is the custom now in France.

CHAPTER II

To one who loves Gothic architecture there are few cathedrals more interesting than the cathedral of Amiens. It was built in 1220 to 1288, — the sixty-eight years of work of the two bishops Everard, who founded it, and Godfrey, who carried it to completion and consecrated it.

The name of the architect is preserved, which is not always the case with Gothic builders. Robert of Luzarches was the designer, and Thomas de Cermont and his son Rénauet completed the building. All honor to them, for they have achieved one of the Gothic wonders of the world.

If the original plan had been carried out, the cathedral of Amiens would be without a peer among Gothic churches. Unfortunately, its exterior is sadly marred by a wooden spire which is so far too small for the church that it seems quite ridiculous, and it is marred also by the failure to complete the two western towers, which were meant to culmi-

5

nate in spires.   The exterior is hurt also by the
too close crowding around it of small buildings.   It
is not possible from any point of view to get an adequate idea of the whole church.   When these criti-
cisms are made, as unfortunately they must be, there
is nothing more to say that does not tell of almost
unlimited admiration.

To convey in words the overpowering effect of the
façade is not possible.   It stands quite alone, in my
mind, among all Gothic façades I know, easily sur-
passing all the others.   Here is the very essence of
the Gothic builder's art.   Here the exquisite lines
of his construction blend in the most perfect harmony
with the superb richness of his ornamentation.   Mr.
Ruskin says that those who built the Gothic churches
really believed they were building dwelling-places
for Christ, and they wished to make them as com-
fortable and beautiful for Him as they could.   The
façade of Amiens certainly bears out this idea, for
the central figure in it is Christ, called "Le Bon
Dieu d'Amiens," who welcomes all who come to
enter its portals and gives them His benediction.

But at first the figures are not noticed individu-
ally.   Arch upon arch, pinnacle above pinnacle,
column above column, pier above pier, its vanishing
lines lost at last in the heavens above, the wondrous
façade bursts upon the astonished eye in an over-

THE CATHEDRAL OF AMIENS

powering grandeur, a wealth of sculpture, an exquisite grace of line and composition, unlike anything
else in all architecture. And when the dazzled
sight has become somewhat accustomed to the full
blaze of this Gothic splendor, when the mind, irresistibly led at first to aspiration, can rejoice in the
beauties that help make the wondrous whole, then
comes the thought, "What spirit was it that inspired
him who did this, and how can he move men thus
through all these ages?" And the mind, answering,
says it is easy to see that perfect honesty of construction and perfect beauty are not far apart. The great
rose window could not be without the strong support
of buttresses that permitted so large openings in such
lofty walls.

Massive solid piers must give strong foundation
for spires that are to touch the clouds, and as the
piers rise higher and higher, and less and less supporting work is to be done, they become lighter and
lighter, vanishing one by one into pinnacles, until at
last the eye is led to the one supreme pinnacle,—the
nearest point toward the heavens the builder's skill
could reach. This utmost touch of the spire is not
here as Robert of Luzarche meant it should be, but
all the lower lines are eloquent of it. In their
own beauty of form and thought they point to the
beauty's consummation, until the completed spire

is seen in a dream, almost, as Robert must have seen it.

But graceful lines and forms were not enough, however inspiring they might be. The portal of the house of God must be beautiful in every part. About the door must be the saints and angels who surround the Lord. The beauties of God's flowers and vines and leaves must lend adornment to these columns and enrich these arches. Thus the sculptor and the cunning carver help the builder. In the great central portal the apostles and saints stand reverently, but with most simple dignity, about their Master. Each figure has its niche in the recessed doorway, and as all stand upon the same level,—and the same order is preserved in the side portals,—the whole forms one long procession of apostles, martyrs, and saints on the Saviour's right hand and on His left, reaching from one side of the vast façade to the other. Above the Saviour's figure is told in stone the thought these pious builders had about the last judgment. Many another scene or story from the Scriptures is here upon the recessed arches and the great bases of the piers, nor is one spot left without its ornament or its sacred figure, excepting such as should be left unornamented in order that grace and strength and beauty of construction might quite plainly be seen.

Far above the saints and apostles who stand about the porches is another long procession, reaching from one side to the other of the façade. These are the kings of Judah, and very majestic and king-like do they seem. At first one might think these should not occupy a higher position than the others, but only a second thought is needed to show that the architect was correct in thus placing them. He wished to put that which was most sacred, that which had most to teach, where it could most easily be seen and best impress its lesson. The kings were not so holy as the saints, and, while they give great dignity to the structure as they stand there apparently helping to support it, there is no need that each of them should tell his life story, while there is the utmost need that Christ and His disciples should speak most plainly and directly to the people. Therefore the kings are placed so high. The points of the portals are crowned with angels, the central one Gabriel, who holds the trumpet that is to voice the last summons. These seem to bring together all the lesson of the sacred story, and tell what its meaning is, and how it shall end in a heavenly home for those who love and worship.

Beside the beautiful lines and forms, the delicate aerial pinnacles and the sumptuous richness of the ornamental sculpture as well as its suggestion of all that is most sacred, there is another feature in the exterior of Amiens hardly less remarkable though not very easily to be studied except from above, and that is the flying buttresses. These are the distinctive feature of Gothic architecture, more truly so even than the pointed arch, and to make them beautiful was the Gothic architect's greatest triumph in one way, because they were not put there for beauty but for the necessary strength of construction. These of Amiens, however, are beautiful. They are pierced with arches and made as light as they can be consistently with the strength they must have. They seem like myriad long arms, as graceful as they are strong, that hold the temple in a firm and tender embrace. They would be like the hundred-handed giant of old if they were not as beautiful as they are strong.

All this is only the exterior. The chief glory of Amiens is within. The wonderful façade is but a gateway, after all, developed into its harmonious beauty because of the thought of a welcoming entrance that might invite worshippers to God's house, and bid them come thither with a humble and a serious heart yet knowing well that peace awaits them within.

One who loves beautiful things, and wishes to know enough about them to have them leave a lasting impression on the mind, will not ask for the custodian when he enters this church. He will avoid that person and every one else and seek to be quite alone, without any words for a long time, hoping that the whole building may tell to him its secret of beauty without confusion of impressions or that waste of mental energy that must come from an effort to comprehend at the same time the vast things and the small ones.

The outside only surrounds the dwelling-place of Christ. Within is the real home, as these builders thought about it, and he who built this cathedral certainly had this idea very close to his heart. The sacred place, sacred beyond all others, is the choir where the high altar stands. About it are the chapels which were the dwelling-places of the saints who were accounted worthy to live so near their Master.

It is for this reason that the choir and apse of Amiens are so superb. At first one does not seek any reason why it should be as it is, but is simply overwhelmed by the majesty, the grace, and the beauty of it. There is no other Gothic choir like this in the impression it gives of vast height. Though that of Beauvais is higher, it does not produce the same effect because the church is unfin-ished. There is no dome to surmount Amiens cathedral, no great tower like that of Canterbury, no lantern as at Burgos — simply and only the Gothic columns and arches spring in unbroken and exquisite lines from floor to ceiling. One *must* look upward even as if the heavens were opened above him. It seems like that. Whence comes that light from above? Is it all glass there, window above window from aisle to clerestory, from clerestory to the very utmost point of this great upward-reaching of the arches?

It scarcely seems possible that so much light can come through all the wall from foundation to pinnacle of so great a building. But so it is. The builder meant the light of heaven to shine upon the Saviour's home. He meant, too, that the light should come there softly in subdued radiance, that it might not be too glaring, and that it should be beautiful with red and purple and yellow, suggesting gratitude and praise for Him who made the rainbow, and by its potent charm inviting all to come and worship in the sacred place.

After long looking in mute admiration, after communion with the spirit of worship that pervades it all, one comes at last to understand what the builder meant. The buttresses outside were for this, that there might be light within, and these towering columns in majestic procession from nave to transept, from transept to choir and apse, are there to hold on high a canopy over the holy place.

As the meaning becomes more plain, the charm of the beauty is more keenly felt, because it is the beauty of symmetry, of perfect, orderly development from a preconceived idea, and that idea the highest known to man, — the thought of absolute, devoted worship.

Mr. Ruskin says of this church in his "Bible of Amiens": "The outside of a French cathedral, except for its sculpture, is always to be thought of as the wrong side of the stuff in which you find how the threads go that produce the inside, or right side, patterns; and if you have no wonder in you for that choir, and its encompassing circlet of light, when you look up to it from the cross centre, you need not travel any farther in search of cathedrals, for the waiting-room of any station is a better place for you: but if it amaze you and delight you at first, then the more you know of it the more it will amaze. For it is not possible for imagination and mathematics together to do anything nobler or stranger than that procession of window, with material of glass and stone, nor anything which shall look loftier with so temperate and prudent measure of actual loftiness. . . . From the unhewn block set on end in the Druids' bethel to this Lord's house and blue

vitrailed gate of heaven, you have the entire course
and consummation of the northern religious builder's
passion and art." The same author calls Amiens
"the first virgin perfect work — the Parthenon of
Gothic architecture."

There is much more in the interior of this church
beside its wonderful effect as a whole. There is a
choir whose wood-carving is equalled by no other in
Europe except that of Cordova. A marvel it is in
itself, and yet so perfectly subordinated in its exterior lines to the church, that it helps rather than
hinders the general effect. This is not often true
of elaborate choirs. The carving here seems to grow
naturally from the great stone columns. It is the
foliage of the forest or the vine that seems to love
to cling about such noble tree trunks. The ornamental effect of it is more beautiful, but not more
interesting, than the stories its figures tell about
what happened in the Jewish days and in the time
of Christ. There are more than three thousand of
these figures. They are beautiful, deliciously quaint,
and always suggestive of the story they mean to tell,
although they are by no means perfect from the
technical point of view.

Curious stories are told about the artists who
made this carving. Trupin was the chief of them,
and he was an artist indeed. Yet he received but

a few pennies a day for his work. His apprentices were paid still less. Some only received three cents a day. What artist would work in these days for such wages? It must be remembered, however, that the penny then would fully equal the shilling now in purchasing power.

This whole choir, with all its masterpieces of carving in figures and decorative work, cost about two thousand dollars, and it gave employment to six or eight good workmen for fourteen years. If this sum should represent ten times as much in actual value to-day, it still seems scarcely possible that such work could be done for such a price. The groups of figures are so numerous and so complicated that any detailed description of them would be uninteresting except to a student. In the smaller figures there is a good deal of a kind of grotesque humor. The portraits of the artists are curiously brought in. They seem almost like caricatures, and yet the faces are so lifelike that they must be good likenesses.

Mr. Ruskin says of it: "It is tastefully developed, flamboyant, just past the fifteenth century, and has some Flemish stolidity mixed with the playing French fire of it; but wood-carving was the Picard's joy from his youth up, and, so far as I know, there is nothing else so beautiful cut out of the goodly trees of the world. Sweet and young-grained oak it is: oak trained and chosen for such work, sound now as four hundred years since. Under the carver's hand it seems to cut like clay, to fold like silk, to grow into living branches, to leap like living flame. Canopy crowning canopy, pinnacle piercing pinnacle — it shoots and wreathes itself into an enchanted glade, inextricable, imperishable, fuller of leafage than any forest, and fuller of story than any book."

On the outside of the choir and in the two transepts are some most quaint and curious bas-reliefs. They illustrate scenes from the lives of St. Firmin and St. Salve, the patron saints of Amiens, the life of John the Baptist, the history of St. James the great, and the expulsion of the money-changers from the temple. These are almost as interesting as the wooden carvings of the choir, though by no means so beautiful.

A part of the head of John the Baptist is said to be here. There must be, I suppose, documents of great length to prove its genuineness, but I had no opportunity to examine them.

The graves of the two bishops who built this church are marked by two of the most remarkable bronze monuments in France. It is said that only two others remain equal to these, — the monuments to the children of St. Louis at St. Denis. The others were destroyed at the time of the Revolution.

It is well that the monuments of those who built the first perfect temple to God in France should remain here undisturbed, and it is fitting that the last thought as one leaves this glorious church should be one of thankfulness to the noble, self-sacrificing, loving, and pious bishops, whose lifelong efforts achieved so mighty a task, and whose earnest hope it was that blessings should come to man from their church long ages after they had gone to their rest.

c

CHAPTER III

BEAUVAIS AND CHARTRES

THE first sight of the cathedral of Beauvais is disappointing. The building is out of proportion — far too high for its length. The reason is that the Beauvais architect attempted far more than he could achieve, partly because his piers were not sufficient for their work, and partly, also, because the purse of the little town was by no means long enough to carry out his design even if it could have been possible under the most favorable conditions to erect the building as he planned, which is certainly very doubtful.

To surpass the apse of Amiens in height and bring still more light into the building with even less use of masonry and larger openings for stained glass was a task which perhaps no architect of those days — not even a Gothic one — could have achieved. The result of the attempt was partial failure. A large part of the building tumbled down, and the rest had to be strengthened by the insertion of

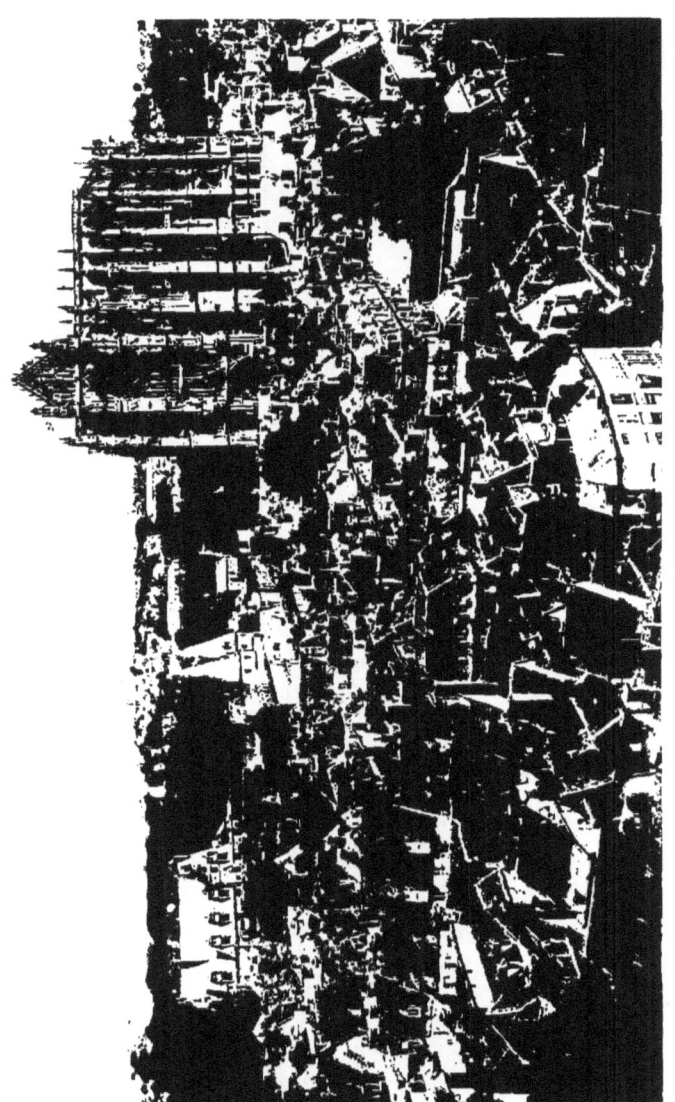

THE CATHEDRAL OF BEAUVAIS

piers not in the architect's design. Then came the other collapse of the finances, and the church was never built at all beyond the transepts, and even these were a later addition. Ambition here overleaped itself, and the attempt to surpass Amiens resulted in so complete a failure that the church of Beauvais seems now from the outside almost like a ruin.

Yet its choir is the loftiest in the world in a Gothic cathedral, considerably higher than that of Amiens. In this choir are three tiers of windows, the lower ones about the chapels, the next in the clerestory, and the third touching with their pointed arches the very roof itself. It is not easy to believe that even the smallest of these windows would seem very large in most churches, while the towering ones above that almost reach the roof would be far too high for any but the very largest buildings.

The same general plan is adopted as at Amiens, yet the effect is not so perfect because the lines of support are not so plainly to be seen. The dizzy height is attained, but at the cost of symmetry and with an uneasy suggestion of insecurity. Some one has well said of the cathedrals of Amiens and Beauvais that "Amiens seems a giant in repose, while Beauvais is a colossus on tip-toe." The vast height is not the only wonder of this choir and apse and these transepts. The stained glass is very fine, especially the lower windows of the chapels about the high altar, which glow with brilliant yellow, amethyst, and topaz and have many a story to tell about the lives of the saints. Sometimes a certain grotesqueness invades even the stained glass. That is not the case in the cathedral at Beauvais, but there is a remarkable example of it in another church in the town, — the very ancient church of St. Étienne.

There is a window here containing what is called the " Tree of Jesse," which is certainly one of the most extraordinary examples of stained glass work that can be found anywhere. In the lower part of the window are nine divisions. Poor old Jesse lies placidly slumbering in the middle one of the three lower divisions. Two great tree trunks grow, — one from each of his sides and reach over into the divisions of the window at his right and his left. Here they blossom into a king for every pane of the window, and more curious examples of royalty it would be hard to imagine. They are all splendidly arrayed, though there might be a question as to their choice of garments.

Solomon is much the funniest. He has on a poke bonnet of the most pronounced New England type, though brilliantly yellow in color, and with a crown on top of it. There is an immense jewel under the bonnet just over his forehead. Why it is there, or how it came there, no one can tell. There is a mixture of splendor and ludicrousness about him that would make an anchorite laugh.

King David is but little better off in the way of dress, but his big harp gives him a kind of seemly occupation, and is a little more in keeping with his life and character than any article in the most unfortunate costume of his son.

Above them all is an immense white lily, the topmost blossom of the tree, from the midst of whose petals emerges the Virgin, with a blaze of glory about her.

In the companion window on the right are scenes from the Last Judgment. There is a violently red devil, with a full equipment of horns, hoofs, and tail, who is holding open the huge mouth of a brilliantly green dragon, with an enormous, protruding blue eye. Into this mouth lesser devils are thrusting the unfortunate souls of the wicked as fast as they can cram them down. The dragon's capacity for eating without swallowing seems to be almost unlimited.

Strangely enough, these windows, when seen from a distance, are very beautiful in color, and there is some really good composition in them.

There are many other interesting places in Beauvais, some of them strikingly picturesque, but it will be more interesting to contrast the stained glass of Chartres with that of this half-finished, but most impressive, cathedral.

In its stained glass Chartres is certainly one of the most beautiful churches in the world. One hundred and sixty windows of perfect form and color made at the time when this exquisite art was at the very acme of its perfection! No one who has not seen it can even imagine the glory of them. The Gothic architect always worked for this effect of light. For this were the columns made as slender as possible, the stonework as delicate and light as it could be and still stand strong; for this were the buttresses and flying buttresses made that the walls might stand firm even although they seem to be almost all of glass. The reason for this method of construction can easily be known in every Gothic church, but the actual effect of it can hardly be appreciated anywhere else in the same way as at Chartres.

This, then, is a new impression — something that has been dreamed of but never really seen before — this magnificent effulgence of gorgeous yet subdued color that tells why Gothic aisles were "pictured aisles." How can it be described? In other

THE CATHEDRAL OF CHARTRES

churches the imagination has put into the windows
the colors that must have been meant to be there,
but at Chartres they are really before the eye, and
they surpass the dream. Here is the perfect blend-
ing of color and light. In how many different ways
it can be produced! It is a revelation. The windows are not alike except in their perfect beauty.
In some red predominates, in others blue, in others
again a most delicious amber. Forms, figures,
designs, combinations — all are infinitely varied,
and yet by some marvel of art all produce an
overwhelming effect of the magnificence of color,
beautiful in itself, but illuminated and made to live
by the sun.

It is useless to tell about the designs of the
different windows, because these must be studied
out with care and difficulty even in the church
itself. They do not count at all in the general
effect, although it is interesting to know that many
of these glorious windows were given to the church
by guilds of trade in the city, and each guild that
gave one sought to commemorate itself by putting
some thought of its trade into the design of the
window.

The armorers, and the shoemakers, the weavers,
the workers in many an industrial art, are here
remembered by their gifts. But fine as it is to

think how these trades-unions wished to make
their church noble and beautiful, it must be con-
fessed that they are hardly thought of beneath the
windows of Chartres. The general effect is too
superb to permit of lingering on any study of detail
for one who must take away only an impression
because he cannot stay long enough to study the
whole design carefully. One thought, however, is
here impressed upon the mind as perhaps nowhere
else among the Gothic churches, and that is the
thought of the place that stained glass holds as a
distinguishing characteristic of Gothic architecture.
It used to be said that the pointed arch determined
this style. Afterward the architects concluded that
the buttress and the flying buttress really distinguish
Gothic from other kinds of building. Perhaps as
true a definition as any may be the giving as much
space in the walls as possible to stained glass.

Chartres certainly stands clearly out with its
testimony that such was the principal aim of the
architect who planned this building so wondrously
illuminated.

CHAPTER IV

THE cathedral of Tours has a beauty quite its
own, different from Amiens, Beauvais, or Chartres,
or any of the others. The beauty of its façade
and its stained glass are its greatest charms, although the nave is very fine, and the peculiar
arrangement of windows over the west portal is
almost unique, and, from the inside, exceedingly
beautiful.

In the façade the richness of what might be called
decorated lines is simply extraordinary. The interlacing arches, points, and pinnacles are so numerous
that the eye can hardly follow them all in the course
of their orderly architectural development. There
used to be the ornament of niches filled with saints
and kings. The niches are there, but the statues are
not, for the Revolution swept these away. If the
architect's original design had been carried out and
his work not disturbed, this façade would be in some
ways even richer than that of Amiens. The construc-

tive part is all here, even nearly to the top of the
towers, and the beauty of it is marvellous.

The loss of the statues is pitiful because of the
sad emptiness of the vacant niches. The sculptures
might not have been great works of art, but even
if they were far from great they are needed to complete this façade of Tours cathedral.

There is another trouble, which is that the towers
are in the Renascence manner, which does not harmonize with the Gothic. Still these tower-tops are
so far above the rest that they interfere but little
with the general effect — less, in fact, than if they had
not been completed at all, as is the case at Amiens.

The first impression of this façade is that the
architect has so harmoniously composed and constructed it that it goes to the heart at the very first
glance with a thought of that upward springing —
that quick look toward *heaven* that only true Gothic
can give. Afterward comes a malediction on the
Revolution. Why were these iconoclasts permitted
to do such dire damage to the greatest works of the
architect's art? At first it seems unpardonable, and
then comes the thought of the provocation. The
blinded dwellers in the cave-houses by the Loire
might well have destroyed anything if they thought
freedom could thus come to them; and surely those
who lived always in the darkness of caves could not

be expected to have a keen appreciation of what is
beautiful to the eye. The priests, who prayed in
vain, if they prayed at all, to save them from their
sufferings, had been not only powerless but oppres-
sive. They had added burdens to the daily life,
promising a reward beyond but offering little here,
and the saints seemed to share in this view of the
peasant's life on earth. Therefore the people, once
getting the power, took all into their own hands, and
being perforce blind because of long living in darkness, tore down together the evil and the good, hav-
ing no power of discrimination. Alas! for the façade
of Tours. Alas! for the windows and the monuments.
Alas! for many a noble building gone forever.

Not all the windows of Tours cathedral were destroyed. Many still remain, and they give a glory to
the church. Nearly all those about the lofty choir
are preserved intact, just as they were meant to
be in the architect's design. I do not know why
they were spared in the Revolution; perhaps it was
a "happy accident," such as saved the windows of
St. Ouen. Nor do I know why they have not been
spoken of more enthusiastically, for no description
of them can be adequate without some enthusiasm.
They tell of the lives of the saints whose num-
bers and deeds never cease to be extraordinary.
They also show the coats of arms of two or three

sovereigns of France, and of the city of Tours with its clustered towers.

It is most difficult to understand how such utterly dissimilar and incongruous subjects could have been used by the artist of the windows and wrought into a perfect harmony. It must be that the artist worshipped his art more than he did the saints, or the kings, or the cities, and therefore he subordinated all of them to the effect of color — the very soul and essence of the art of stained glass.

The story of the windows may be found out by patient study, but while so studying the general effect is lost, and this is the chief glory of it. It is a radiant flood of light, and yet it is not full sunlight but light much subdued and softened. It is as if the full rays of the sun were too dazzling for mortal eyes, and therefore the parts of the rays that, joined, make all its whiteness must be taken separately and thus more gently led to the eye, that the beauty of each may be felt in turn — the red, the yellow, the green, the purple, and all the shades of them. If each part alone is so beautiful, a deeper thought is suggested about the glory of the sun ray in which they all are merged. It may be there is some significance in it. It may be the artist thought only of beauty. The effect cannot be wholly analyzed, but it can partly be felt. These windows have their picturesque side,

too, different from their religious and artistic suggestions. When the cardinals and bishops and priests
with all their splendid train were beneath them, and
when the kings and nobles of the land were there
in all the richness of robes of court, or gleaming
armor, what play of color there must have been!
How the tiaras and the crowns and the helmets
would softly glow and gleam as they passed beneath
window after window, each touching them with a
different hue: and as they neared the high altar the
candle-light would add still another color note.

What artist can rightly picture such scenes? Many
have tried but few have succeeded, perhaps because
there is, after all, a key-note of religion beneath all
the gorgeous color, that must be struck if the picture
is to be true. It cannot be thought that such great
and faithful artists as made the windows of Tours
cathedral worked without much religious inspiration.
Their work was consecrated, at least in part, and it
is not possible to understand it without appreciating
to a certain extent the reverent worshipping spirit
that prompted it.

Through these windows come thoughts of God
and the praise of Him, loveliest suggestions of nature's own beauty, and stories and pictures of the
lives that were lived beneath the tender glories of
their softened light.

CHAPTER V

CAEN

WILLIAM THE CONQUEROR and Matilda, his wife, had married contrary to the rules of the Roman Church as to marriages between those related by blood. For this reason they sought absolution from the Pope, and it may be that the great churches at Caen were a part of their penance. Such is the history of the foundation of many a church in France, though the buildings were carried on and brought to completion by those who had nothing to do with the sin of the founders.

William founded the Abbaye aux Hommes, Matilda the Abbaye aux Dames. Both are magnificent churches. They are especially interesting to those who have studied the Gothic architecture of France, and can find here a contrast to that style; for these churches, although not wholly Norman, are partly so, and they show perhaps as well as any others what the Norman church-builder could do. His power is more in strength than in beauty. His people had

THE CASTLE OF FALAISE

conquered others often. Probably he thought they always would conquer. The Gothic architects belonged to a conquering people, too, but they do not express their thoughts of conquest in their churches. On the contrary, they seemed to be seeking the beauty of light. The contrast is interesting.

The Abbaye aux Hommes at Caen has a most imposing façade. There is no sculptured ornament about its porches, and yet it was the inspiration even of such façades as that of Amiens. Here was the strength. Such buildings would stand unless the solid earth beneath them gave way. The Gothic architect took the strength and added the ornament.

The same thought is suggested by the Abbaye aux Dames. The façade is even more imposing than the other, but still there is no ornament such as the Gothic builder always uses. Nevertheless, there is a wonderful grandeur in the building. It seems almost like a fort of religion, built for defence and not at all for attack. Within these solid walls the noble ladies for whom Queen Matilda built the abbaye could live in peace. There could be no entrance for any one who wished to disturb their quietness.

One part of this church, which is similar in position to the choir in Gothic cathedrals, is entirely shut off from the rest of the building. It was here

that those women who had taken the veil worshipped, quite secluded from all the rest of the
world. In the midst of them was, and still is, the
tomb of Matilda herself. How many masses for
the repose of the queen's soul must have been said
around the simple slab of stone a little elevated
above the pavement, that marks the place where
her bones were laid!

The massive character of the Norman architecture
is not well suited to church interiors. It is imposing because of its strength — but it does not admit
enough of the light. The windows, both in the
Conqueror's abbaye and that of his wife, are very
small, except in the parts of the buildings added
later, which are Gothic in style. There would have
been no spires for the façade of the Abbaye aux
Hommes if the Norman builder's work had been
let alone. He did not care any more about spires
than he did about great windows.

Neither aspiration nor light seems to have had
much to do with his plan of building. He was
very Roman in his ways, but he was not imagina-
tive, nor was he poetical. Nevertheless, the great
round arches rising one above the other to the top
of the clerestory are certainly very impressive. It
is a pity that William the Conqueror's church should
ever have been touched by a Gothic architect.

There should have been no spires, no apse with pointed lancet-windows. It should all have been left massive, strong, without ornament and dimly lighted. This Norman spirit was grim enough, and certainly here at Caen it should find its fitting embodiment in stone; for it was here that the great soldier's bones were laid, who perhaps better than any other man expressed in his life the essential typical qualities of the Norman character.

It is a great pity, too, that the soldier-king's bones were not allowed to remain in the church he built. His tomb is there, but it is empty, and has long been so. The Calvinists threw his ashes to the winds. It seems a strange irony of fate that the man so irresistible in his life should have been quite deserted at his death, and even his remains not allowed to lie in peace. The great Conqueror was buried by the private charity of one of his knights, and during the funeral services a peasant demanded money for the grave, which, as he claimed, was on his land, and had never been paid for. The bishop had to pay him before the funeral ceremonies could be completed.

Caen is also fascinating because it shows so clearly the growth of the Gothic from the Norman architecture. One of the most beautiful Gothic spires in France is that of the church of St. Pierre. One

D

passes it in going from one abbaye to the other. It is
an absolutely perfect example of early Gothic; quite
as beautiful in its lines even as the apse of Amiens.
Mr. Ruskin would say that no higher praise could be
given to a Gothic building, and he would be quite
correct in saying so. Nevertheless, even such praise
is deserved by the spire of St. Pierre. It is not richly
ornamented, for it is of the early style just after the
Norman, but it rises arch upon arch and pinnacle
upon pinnacle, to the vanishing point against the
sky with that grace, that uplifting spirit, only
known to the Gothic builders.

That first experience of Caen is hardly to be had
elsewhere. To pass from the great Norman church
of William to the equally great Norman church of
his wife, and on the way to see an exquisite spire in
quite a different style: it is rare, indeed, to see so
many and so different noble monuments of religious
building so closely grouped together.

But the charm and interest of Caen are not ex-
hausted even by the two abbayes and the wonderful
spire of St. Pierre. There are most interesting examples of the Renascence architecture also, especially
the old Bourse, the court of which is extremely
picturesque. When the architecture of the time of
Francis I. is added to that of the Norman days and
the time of the Gothic building, it would seem as

if the cup of interest for an architect would be full to overflowing.

Only a short distance from Caen is Falaise, where William the Conqueror was born. Here is one of the most interesting of the Norman castles of France. It was built like the châteaux of Touraine, on the top of a hill, but it was more strongly fortified than most of the castles by the Loire. It was a place for war. Luxury, ease, even comfort, had no part in it. The immense *donjon* keep is as stern as was the Bastille. The tower of Talbot beside it is just as stern, though taller and more beautiful in form. There were oubliettes in it and dungeons.

These great towers look down upon the valley of the Ante, a little stream which does its best to fertilize the land about it, and succeeds, as the French streams have a habit of doing.

Duke Robert of Normandy stood one day in the *donjon* at what they call a window, and he looked down at the stream and the valley far below. In the water was bathing Arlette, the daughter of a tanner. There were many tanners in Falaise then, and there are many now. The duke was charmed with the young girl, and she became William the Conqueror's mother. The room in which he was born is little better than a cell. It has, however, a chimney, and that must have seemed quite luxurious in those days.

There was a recessed place for the bed, and some
other recesses in the masonry, probably intended for
toilet articles.   There could have been little comfort
about it, though possibly the walls were hung with
tapestry.   In this room, which seems like a cave in
a vast mountain of masonry, the conqueror of England was born.   In the great abbaye he built near by
at Caen his bones were laid to rest, though not allowed to rest there.

The story and the art of Caen and Falaise are
intensely interesting to all who speak the English
language.

CHAPTER VI

In Rouen almost every form of Gothic architecture can be studied as perhaps in no other city. There were at one time thirty-two churches here. One-half were destroyed, mostly at the time of the Revolution. Sixteen remain, and in these can be seen very nearly all the French Gothic architect knew about church building; and in the Palais de Justice can equally well be seen what he could do in civic architecture.

The cathedral is wonderfully interesting and quite different, especially in the façade, from any of the other great Gothic cathedrals. The contrast between this and other noted façades comes from the very curious fact that although the ancient façade was very beautiful, George d'Amboise, the famous cardinal of Louis XII.'s time, thought he could improve it by adding pinnacles and porches and the most elaborate sculptured ornament. All this lavish wealth of ornamentation was put on later by him. It formed no part of the original design, and yet it is wonderfully beautiful.

The critics may talk as they please about too great elaboration, too close an approach to a debased style of Gothic. Nevertheless, the façade is one of the most interesting in Europe, and the porches at each side are no less remarkable. They are hardly to be surpassed anywhere in richness of ornament, and they are beautiful in form also. The beauty of their delicate traceries and the effect of the myriad statues and carvings that adorn them are only enhanced by contrast with the severer early pointed style which is seen in the lower part of the towers at either side of the façade.

But beautiful, wonderful, as the cathedral is, the church of St. Ouen far surpasses it, perhaps because it is one of the very few Gothic churches in Europe carried to completion upon the original design. It may be added that it is one of the very few that are entirely finished. The first stone of St. Ouen was laid in 1318, and the principal part of the church was finished before 1500. That is a very short history for a Gothic church. The two spires of the façade were added later, but they are at least in sympathy with the design of the architect, though not quite as he would have wished. If one dreamed of pure Gothic at the very moment when richest ornament was combined

THE PALAIS DE JUSTICE AT ROUEN

with purest line, he would find the realization of his dream at St. Ouen. There is no Gothic interior less interfered with by choir screen or chapels. Certainly there is none more perfect in unity of style. These technical words mean little when one tries to suggest a thought of beauty. The secret of the beauty of St. Ouen is, as I think, closely connected with its columns. They rise together with the same lines and forms, and when they can all be seen from one end of the vast church to the other, it is better than if some were round and some square as happens sometimes, and far better than it would be if a great choir screen, however beautifully carved and ornamented, prevented a complete view of the church from end to end.

There is a custodian here, called the " Swiss," perhaps from some idea about the Pope's guard. He told me that he had taken Mr. Ruskin many times about the church of St. Ouen, within and without, and that he had heard him say there was no purer or finer example of Gothic architecture in existence. But these people who live in the church and point out its beauties every day to those who come to see it must be pardoned for a little enthusiasm sometimes. It may be that Mr. Ruskin himself will have to beg forgiveness for the same fault.

This church has a strange history. There were

three churches before this one on the same site. Of
the latest of these three, built by a nephew of William the Conqueror, only one small, round Norman
tower remains. The present church was once an
armory and a stable at the same time. This was in
the days of the French Revolution.

Curiously enough, such use of the church was not
a misfortune, but a good happening. In order that
there might not be draughts from the sides on the
armory fires, the stained glass windows were left un-
touched, and because the armorers, whose trade was
similar to that of the iron-workers, greatly admired
the hammered-iron screen about the choir, that was
not disturbed either. Thus two of the most exquisite works of art in St. Ouen were preserved by what
some would call an accident, and others the hand of
Providence.

Another curious result of the use of the church as
an armory is the effect of the smoke of the forges on
the columns. This has given to the stone a bluish-
gray color, very peculiar and extremely beautiful.
The natural color of the stone was probably similar
to that of the columns of the cathedral, which are
almost yellow. St. Ouen, then, is one of the few
churches which were helped by the French Revolution.

The central tower of this church is one of the

most beautiful in Europe, the only one that surpasses it being that of Burgos. The cap of the
tower is in the form of the crown of Normandy,
and its ornamentation is mostly the fleur-de-lis, as
was that of the crown itself.

But St. Ouen, with its columns and its tower, is
not the only work of the Gothic art that is to be
seen at Rouen. There is also the Palais de Justice.
This most beautiful building shows that the same
manner of construction that has been used with such
wonderful effect in the churches may also be applied
successfully to quite a different use.

The town halls of Antwerp and Bruges are perhaps
the most perfect examples of this use of the Gothic
principles, but the Palais de Justice at Rouen is not
far behind them in beauty. It is built about a court
of which it surrounds three sides. The other side is
left open for an entrance and to give light to the
rooms within. The building is not high—two stories
only in some parts, and three in others. It is not
imposing, nor is there any effort for such an effect,
but it is beautiful in a way most wonderful when
one thinks what problem of usefulness the architect
had to solve before he could think at all about the
beauty of it. He had to provide both great and small
rooms within, and all were to be well lighted. The
building as a whole was to be symmetrical, and pleas-

ing in form and proportion. These were the first
things to be thought of. After that came the question about where the ornament would best be placed,
and what kind of ornament it should be.

The architect chose to centralize the exterior ornament upon the piers at each side of the windows,
and the pinnacles surmounting them. These are exquisitely carved and greatly varied in size and form.
The judges needed a small room into which they
might retire for deliberation. To meet this need, and
at the same time vary the lines of his façade, the
architect made an oriel window, and he put it in the
centre where its beauty would best be appreciated.
This oriel window is one of the finest examples of
civic Gothic architecture in Europe.

Within this building, whose exterior is so charming,
are noble halls and other rooms of great size. One
of these halls is called "La Salle des Pas perdus"—
a free translation of which would be "The Room
where Time is wasted." It means that the lawyers
walked up and down in this hall with their clients,
consulting with them there instead of doing that in
private rooms, as is the custom nowadays. Surely it is
a satire upon the legal profession to call such a place
by a name that is really insulting. The hall itself
is worthy of a better name, for it is lofty, spacious,
beautiful in proportion, and truly Gothic in spirit.

The court room where the trials of criminals take place is very fine. It has a most splendid ceiling of oak — not in the ordinary raftered form, but with most intricate, interlacing beams with pendants a few feet apart which must have been intended to support candelabra, though none are there now. Above the chair of the chief justice, on the wall behind it, is a large crucifix. This is always in a French criminal court, and it is used in the oath taken by the witnesses.

It is a great pity there is no association with Joan of Arc in this magnificent building. Her story touches with poetry, romance, and the spirit of religion, every place which was the scene of any event in her most remarkable life.

She was not tried in the Palais de Justice of Rouen, but in a round tower with a conical top in quite another part of the town. The real tower no longer exists, but it has been replaced by one similar to it on the same spot.

The original tower was part of a castle which has altogether disappeared. Nor can one be sure exactly where this peasant maiden, the saviour of her country, was burned at the stake. There is a fountain in the Place de la Pucelle with a hideous modern statue above, which was once supposed to mark the place, but further investigation has shown that the very spot where she was martyred was not there but a short distance away in the market-place. A tablet of granite with a commemorative inscription has been inserted in the sidewalk by the market upon the spot where it is thought the stake was raised and the fagots piled up about the heroic Maid of Domrémy. It is in the very midst of the busy life of that people whose existence as a nation owed so much to her devotion.

Impressive as this thought is, it is more impressive still to think that a monument has been raised to her honor upon the hill-top of Bon Secours which overlooks Rouen, and that people visit it as they would go to the shrine of a saint.

A more commanding, beautiful, and impressive site for such a monument could hardly be imagined. The river Seine, broad and strong, flows slowly by the foot of the hill. It seems to wish to linger there and lift a mirrored form to answer like an echo to the almost speaking spirit of the statue above.

Below rise the spires and towers of the cathedral, of St. Ouen, St. André, and the tower of the maiden's trial. These come from the olden time. There are chimneys too, many of them suggesting the busy industries which might not have been there now unless Joan of Arc had done what she was called upon to do.

The monument itself is quite elaborate in construction. There is a chapel, and above this rises the structure in which the statue stands. There are two smaller structures of similar character on either side, in which are figures of saints. There is no need of describing anything but the statue itself, which is one of the greatest works of the art of sculpture that has been produced even by this wonderful school of France — the third distinctively great one of the world. Barrias was the sculptor, and he was certainly inspired in his work with some spirit that has made this statue more alive even than ordinary people are. It is not the living Joan of Arc alone — it is what she did, what she thought, all the trial and trouble of her time, and the spiritual power that prevailed not only in the battles but at the stake.

This simple maid, this peasant girl of Domrémy, believed in her God and her country, and because of her belief came her success. It is the power of faith. There was courage with it, too — nor did that fail even when the flames rose about her. She asked her confessor to hold the crucifix higher, that she might see it above the smoke. The Cardinal of Winchester, who was looking on, became impatient, and asked the priest who held the crucifix whether he meant to keep them there until after dinner-time. The truth was with the woman unjustly condemned

— not with the sneering prelate. It is no wonder
the French wish to have Joan of Arc canonized.
There are few saints in all the long calendar who
better deserve the halo of their sainthood.

"Oh! Captive maid upon thy hill-top lone
  Keeping perpetual vigil o'er the land
  Thy young heart broke to save, forever stand
  Clothed in immortal whiteness, and o'ershone
  By the wide heavens — a victim to atone
  By thy pure consecration for the crime
  And shame, and madness of wild, warring time.
  Yea, stand through all the ages to command
  From out the vast unseen by the strong plea
  That clasps those fettered hands, a bright array
  Of holy shapes, whose white wings silently
  Shall lead thy dear, loved land upon her way
  To victory divine on fields of life
  Where Light and Darkness wage supernal strife."

CHAPTER VII

THE two dearest places in France to poets, artists, and historians are Carcassonne and Mont St. Michel. The two do not greatly resemble each other. Their spirit is quite different, but it seems like going into another century to visit either of them. The marvellous resurrection of a life long past which is seen in both is partly the work of M. Viollet-le-Duc who restored them, and it is certainly due in part also to the wisdom and patriotism of the French which made them willing to restore their ancient monuments however great the cost might be.

Mont St. Michel rises from the sea between Avranches and Cancale. It is very near the border-line between the Norman and the Breton, and it seems as if both peoples had helped in the building of it because of its wonderful union of strength and picturesqueness. It was an abbey once, one of the richest and most powerful in France, and afterward it was a fort. Now it is an historical monument, visited by throngs of people every day.

47

There are hours when Mont St. Michel does not
rise from the sea at all, but is surrounded by a vast
waste of gray sand which the receding tide has left
bare. It seems, then, far removed from the habitations of men, built for some mysterious purpose in
a sad and lonely place to which none would wish
to come. It is most grand and impressive in such
a solitude. Strangely enough, when the tide comes
in, and the place is surrounded by water, this feeling
of complete isolation disappears. The reason must
be that it seems natural to approach places in boats,
while it is not usual to build great churches and
castles in the midst of a desert of wet sand. This
peculiar situation, now in the midst of rippling
water, now encircled by a great gray sand plain,
gives to Mont St. Michel an interest quite its own, —
enough to make it unique even apart from the wonderful charm of its architecture.

The historical associations of the place are perhaps
as interesting as anything about it. It was dedicated
to St. Michael, the patron saint of high places, because it happened one day that a Benedictine monk,
Aubert by name, had a vision in which the mighty
conqueror of the dragon appeared to him, and, point-
ing to a rock rising from the sea, said he must found
a monastery there. Aubert did so. He had no
trouble in finding a name for it; for when the saint

MONT ST. MICHEL

pointed to the high rock as the place for the building, he must have meant that the church should be called by his own name. And so it was. Naturally, this monk, Aubert, was made a saint afterwards.

The story of this vision is represented in a very quaint bas-relief over the gateway that gives entrance to the court in front of the old church. Aubert, apparently just awakened, and still half reclining, looks where the finger of the angel points, and there is a great rock, and a lamb grazing on the top of it. Perhaps here begin the contrasts of St. Michel, — the sternness of the towering rock, the gentleness of the lamb, together in the vision of the monk.

Not very long after the abbey was founded, it became a fort as well as a monastery. Rollo, the first Duke of Normandy, took it under his protection, and used it for military purposes. When his descendant, William, went over to conquer England, Mont St. Michel was able to help him with several vessels, doubtless well manned, for the monks knew how to fight in those days, and even some of the bishops too, like Odo, "the fighting bishop of Bayeux," who was William the Conqueror's brother.

Spiritual and military strength seem to have been combined here in about equal proportions for a long time. The monastery had a great reputation for its sanctity, and the fort could not be taken even

D

by Henry V., whose armies had overrun all Normandy after the battle of Agincourt.

The contrasts which are so striking at Mont St. Michel begin to become more and more distinct and sharply defined. The monks were praying and singing and doing penance in the church and the cloisters on the hill-top, where the watchword of their religion was peace, while fierce battle was being waged about the walls and towers and ramparts below.

In those old days the attacking soldiers could not win because of the strength of the place, and, therefore, the monks prayed on in peace. Later, a more insidious foe attacked the reverend brethren, and they were banished because of immorality. They were replaced by another order, and after that came the final conquest of Mont St. Michel, — the conquest of the pilgrims. They came here by the thousand. The old parish church, which is now, and has been for years, the place of worship of the little town below the fortress monastery, is fairly full of the banners and votive offerings of those who came from near and from far to worship at this sacred shrine. For them the portcullis was raised, — for them the bridge was lowered. They had welcome entrance where the hosts of Agincourt's hero could not by any means enter.

But the brave defenders who resisted Henry V. must not be forgotten. They were great soldiers. Louis d'Estouteville was their chief, and there were many noble knights with him.

There is a house near the parish church, — the church of the pilgrims, — the house of Du Guesclin, the best and bravest among the French chivalry of his time. It is now a museum, where many curious things are to be seen, among them Du Guesclin's library, consisting of a few enormous volumes resembling in size and shape the old missals and service-books of the church that one finds in the sacristies of the oldest cathedrals. Here are the coats of arms of d'Estouteville himself, and of all those who helped him defend the place against the English during two sieges, in 1417 and 1423.

Close by these warlike emblems are the "Treasures of St. Michael," crowns and heraldic collars, vessels for holding the sacrament when it was elevated before the people, and many other such things — all of them gifts of pilgrims. These are all modern, for the irreverent soldiers of the Revolution despoiled the ancient monastery of all its vast treasure of gold and jewels. Here, as elsewhere in this singular place, the implements of religion and of war are side by side.

All this is only a preface to Mont St. Michel.

The real entrance is not that at the end of the long causeway that leads from the road to Pontorson. That gateway only pierces the walls about the base of the rock, — walls tower-crowned, like those of Aigues-Mortes, but not so high nor defended by so many towers as those of St. Louis's seaport. Within these were lines of ramparts which wind about the hill, gradually ascending until the monastery is reached. These are fortified in all ways known to mediæval warfare. It is plain the monks did not trust their defence to the spiritual arm any more than did the Bishop of Carcassonne. There was always the idea of war about Mont St. Michel — possibly because the saint himself was so great a conqueror.

The long ascent of the winding ramparts would be tiresome were it not that there is so much of interest to be seen at every step of the way.

At last comes the real entrance, — a great arch built at the top of a steep stone stairway. Strangely enough, although it is the real entrance to the wonders of the monastery, it opens into the Salle des Gardes, the soldiers' room. This is a most curious apartment built on different levels connected by flights of steps and with an immense fireplace in the lower part.

But when this martial hall is passed, the path leads

steeply up between the buildings of the bishop and
the chief officers of the monastery on one side, and
the church on the other. There are bridges connecting the two to give private entrance to the
church for the officiating clergy, and below the
bridges were portcullises to help the soldiers defend
them.

Penetrating farther and passing below the bridges
of the priests, there is no longer anything to suggest
a thought of battle, any more than there is in Carcassonne's glorious cathedral.

On entering the church, upon the very top of the
rock there comes a vision of columns and arches,
Norman and Gothic, almost overwhelming at first,
so imposing are the massive piers and round arches
of the Norman, so inspiring the graceful, upreaching
lines of the Gothic builder's work.

The comparison of the magnificent stately Norman
nave and the exquisite delicate Gothic choir and transepts is most instructive, but it is not so interesting as
that between the crypt and the cloisters. It would
be well if these could be seen one directly after the
other, but this can hardly be, for they are in different
parts of the vast building. The crypt is under the
church; the cloisters crown the Gothic "Marvel"
on the other side of the rock. Nevertheless, they
should be kept together in thought, for the contrast

between them is a never-to-be-forgotten lesson in architecture.

The columns of the crypt are so vast and so numerous that the Norman architect seems to have thought he was called upon to support not one but a hundred churches. So enormous and so close together are they that the place is dark. Only after the eye becomes accustomed to the gloom is it possible to realize the grandeur, power, and beauty of these columns. They are great tree trunks that begin to branch out in the vault of the crypt, but tower higher in the columns of the church until their topmost branches intertwine in the arches of the nave and the transept and the choir amid the sunshine of the painted windows.

Far above in the full light of day are the cloisters — one of the most exquisite, delicately graceful, and richly ornamented of all Gothic structures. There is certainly some influence of the Moor upon the architecture here, for the cloistered court strongly resembles the Court of the Lions at the Alhambra. In both the carvings are of the richest beauty and the forms of the columns are similar. It is strange that these styles should come so closely together, for they had no sympathy in motive. It is strange, also, that one of the most fanciful, almost playfully decorated of Gothic buildings should be here in this old Benedictine monastery on the top of a sea-girt rock. It seems as if some magician's wand had touched the cold stone, and made the stems of plants spring from it, and then these blossomed of themselves into all manner of lovely foliage and flowers. When this beautiful thing had come to pass, the prayerful, earnest spirit of man added figures and groups that might tell stories of the life of Him who had taught the highest. The charm of it all is not to be told in words, but it comes back in dreams to those who have seen it.

I have said that these cloisters are a part of the "Marvel." Below them is the Salle des Chevaliers, and below that the cellar of the monks, but this is only one-half of the building, for there are three great halls connecting with these, the monks' dormitory, the refectory, and the room for the distribution of alms. The whole six great structures form one building. They have earned the name of "Marvel," partly because of the immense difficulty of building them at all in such a place, and partly on account of the very short time required for their construction, for they were all built in twenty-five years — from 1203 to 1228.

The thirteenth-century Gothic of France is peculiarly fine. These halls partake of its spirit, although they are somewhat later than the purest work of that style.

The Salle des Chevaliers is one of the noblest Gothic halls in Europe, superior, I think, even to the great Hall of the States-General at Blois. Massive round columns support the vaulted roof. They have not clustered columns about them, as in later Gothic work, but they do have beautifully carved capitals, with bold projections from which rise the superb pointed arches of the vault. There are three rows of them, and they make the room seem like three aisles of a great cathedral, and yet they are not near enough together to interfere with the unity of the whole effect. The gray stone is nowhere touched by color, but it is flooded by the sunshine from the windows on the side toward the sea. The impression of it is that here strength, grace, and ornament are joined in perfect proportion.

In this room the superiors of the monastery met and deliberated about its spiritual and worldly affairs. Its name, however, comes from the fact that here Louis XI. founded his order of the " Chevaliers de Mont St. Michel." The decoration of the order was the collar of St. Michael — a very rich necklace, it might be called, which hung low down on the breast, and was made of the scallop shells sacred to the pilgrims of St. James linked together by the cords those pilgrims wore, with a pendent medallion of St. Michael slaying the dragon. The honor of this order was greatly coveted.

The historical suggestions of the room partake of the spirit of Mont St. Michel, because of the startling contrasts. There are the holy fathers sitting among these columns and caring for the needs of the church — there is the crafty, cruel, yet most able king sitting there too, and strengthening his throne by a new order of knighthood, and then there are the knights whom he created gathered there, each wearing his superb collar, and all discussing affairs of state and of war.

The other halls are not so interesting as the cloisters, the church, or the Salle des Chevaliers, but nevertheless they are most impressive, and of very pure and noble architecture. The dormitory of the monks is a grand Gothic room. Its beauty is not disturbed by partitions, for there were no cells in it. The beds were placed side by side all in the one long hall. These monks seem to have been unusually sociable. Not only did they all sleep in the same room, but they ate in the same room, too, — the refectory, which is below the dormitory. This also is an immense hall. One end was partitioned off for a kitchen, and the great chimney pieces where the cooking was done still remain. Below this again is another hall as large as either of the others, in which alms were distributed to the dependents of the monastery.

It is not far from these stately rooms to the dungeons, which were as dark and cruel as the others are full of light and the spirit of devotion. Strange that there should have been an iron cage like that of Cardinal Balue at the very door of the crypt that holds up the church! Strange that dungeon after dungeon, unlighted caves in a cliff of masonry, should be beneath the sacred places where monks prayed and bread was given to the poor! But not stranger perhaps than other mysteries in this inexplicable place. And yet all that we have seen thus far has been under the light of day. Even the dungeons might catch a gleam of it here and there. The cloisters were full of it, and it streamed into the church through the stained glass windows. This full sunlight everywhere is not the light that romantic painters or writers choose. Scott said that no one had seen Melrose Abbey who had not seen it by the light of the moon.

We sat together, talking, late in the evening, thinking not of moon or tide, but of what we had seen during the day. The full moon rose and the tide came in. St. Michael's Mount was surrounded by water. Why not take a boat and row about it?

Down into the streets of the little town we went and at last the boatmen were awakened. They came down the narrow street and we went with them to the beach. The boat was unloosed and we were afloat, not on the waters we know but on those of our dreams. Silently except for the plash of the oar we passed beneath the outer walls whose towers loomed up more grandly in the night. Farther away we went and then we saw the ramparts and the walls silvered by the moon. Farther still we went and the "Marvel" rose above us. The soft, but brilliant light touched every arch, every window, every tower. No one could tell exactly where each hall was, for there is a mystery in moonlight; but it was sure that all were there, and not only that, — the story of them was there. In this almost magical light, with this dreamy sound of the oars' slow plash Mont St. Michel sprang again to life as it could not beneath the full rays of the sun.

Attacking hosts were about it. They were baffled by French heroes. Saints were on the moonlit rock-top — saints from whose visions came all the wonder of it. Prisoners were in the dungeons. There the moon does not shine, but there are deep shadows that tell of the captives' sufferings. There is the martial glory of the fortress, the spiritual ecstasy of the church and the cloister, the moan of the weary prisoner, the commanding majesty of the Knights' Hall.

There is no light in it all now. These vast halls are empty. The vigilant custodians of this great historical monument of France sleep after the arduous labors of the day. There is no sign of life in all the immense fortress-monastery. There is no one on the waters of the rising tide about it. Slowly, rhythmically, the oars plash. Every instant the moon gives a new picture of Mont St. Michel. At last all seems like a dream, and as the boat touches the sand when we come back it is not easy to remember the truth of daylight because of the glamour of this moonlight mystery upon such a place.

It may be that the real truth of it now is not far from dreamland, quite such a picture as could only be seen beneath the moon's rays, for Mont St. Michel is no part of the life of to-day. It is a resurrection of the past. It is the ghost of mediævalism walking abroad, fully to be seen in the moonlight, and in the moonlight alone.

The spirit of times long past forever incarnate in stone, lives upon this rock to tell of heroes and of saints.

CHAPTER VIII

THERE cannot be many places in the world that produce so profound an effect upon the mind,.the imagination, and the sense of beauty as the old walled town of Carcassonne in ancient Languedoc.

Toledo, in Spain, is a walled town too, and one of the most interesting in Europe, but it is far inferior in charm to this French stronghold of days long past. How long past are the days when Carcassonne was founded, or even the time when it had a recognized existence as a city of some importance, no man can tell. Its early history is mostly lost. Enough remains, however, to show that it existed long before the Christian era.

As M. Viollet-le-Duc says, it was in the year 636 of the calendar of Rome that the Roman senate, on the advice of Lucius Crassus, decided to establish a colony in this part of France, and Carcassonne was chosen as one of the chief points for its defence, because it commanded one of the principal roads that led into Spain.

It was in the year 70 B.C. that Carcassonne was placed among the "chosen noble cities." It was then made a citadel, a "castellum," by the Romans. From this time until the fourth century after Christ little is known of its history. Apparently it was a stronghold strong enough to preserve peace in its neighborhood during those centuries, and doubtless the humble folk who lived about it flourished exceedingly, tended their vines and their fields of grain, raised their cattle and horses, and knew little and cared less about the convulsions that were then rending the Roman world to pieces.

But their peace did not endure long, for in the year 350 the Franks took the city, but they were afterward displaced by the Romans. Nearly a century later Theodoric, the king of the Visigoths, took it in his turn from the Romans, and by the treaty made in the year 439 Carcassonne remained in the possession of Theodoric.

From this time on the peaceful days of the place were ended. The Visigoths made it a most important fortress. Clovis laid siege to it in the year 508, but he was unable to take it. The king of the Visigoths still held it.

Then came the Moors, who did take it, and remained masters of it for a long time. They have

CARCASSONNE. PORTE DE L'AUDE AND BISHOP'S TOWER

left one magnificent square tower as their contri-
bution to its defences. Afterward came Louis IX.
and Philip the Bold, Pope Urban II., and many
another who had to do with the history of this
place.

The historical associations of Carcassonne are so
numerous, — they have to do with so many different peoples, — that the first impression about its
history is confused, because it is hard to tell where
the chief emphasis should be placed among all the
scenes of its long story.

Perhaps the siege and capture of it by Simon
de Montfort, Earl of Leicester, the cruel persecutor
of the Albigenses, is one of the most notable events
in its history, although the siege of the place in
1240 by Raymond de Trincavel, the last of the
Vicomtes de Bézier, was hardly less remarkable.
He came very near to capturing the city, but failed
on account of reinforcements sent by the king of
France.

But it is perhaps better, certainly it is pleasanter,
not to study out the ancient history of Carcassonne,
but to live in its atmosphere for a day. Here
one forgets that this is the nineteenth century.
There is nothing that seems to have anything to
do with modern ways of living.

After climbing the steep ascent to the Porte

Narbonnaise, one sees the lofty, crenellated walls, the massive towers pierced with many a loophole for the archers. Is it possible that entrance will be given over this narrow bridge that spans the moat and is flanked by towers of most portentous strength?

At once, almost instinctively, comes a feeling that some shelter must be found for protection against the flights of arrows, the rain of stones and of boiling oil that guard this tremendous gate. It is another world. If it is a dream, it is so real that its impression is more powerful than that of actual life. If it is not a dream, it seems as if it must be, because it is so unlike anything that waking eyes are accustomed to look upon.

This walled town of Carcassonne is built upon a hill-top, and its fortifications follow the lines of the precipices and sloping banks that form the hill. It is like one of Doré's drawings. With black clouds behind its towers and knights in armor riding toward its gates, it would seem almost exactly like one of the illustrations of the "Idylls of the King."

This sternly frowning fortress, grim and strong though it is, looks forth in every direction upon one of the loveliest landscapes in France.

The Aude flows by the foot of the hill, spanned

just below the castle by an ancient and most picturesque bridge with nine massive Romanesque arches. All around in the plain and on the hillsides are vineyards and olive orchards. Far away on the one hand are the Black Mountains, and still farther away on the other are the snow-clad Pyrenees.

But exquisite as the landscape is, it is better not to linger long in looking upon it. There are beautiful views elsewhere, but there is only one Carcassonne.

This place is not only a fortress, but a city. It is easy to forget this in looking at the walls from the outside, because they seem like one gigantic fort intended to dominate all the land it overlooks. Within, however, there is to-day a city. In days gone by there were faubourgs outside the walls, and protected by them, which extended for a considerable distance all about the fortifications. These were, however, destroyed by several princes. Louis IX. destroyed part of them, because the inhabitants had helped Raymond de Trincavel in his siege of the place. The Black Prince burned up all he could of them because he could not take Carcassonne itself. The fact is that he did not attempt to take it. Not even this hero dared attack Carcassonne, which was thought to be and probably was impregnable by mediæval methods of warfare.

F

It is worth remembering that the fortress of Carcassonne successfully resisted the ablest English soldier of his time, the conqueror of France.

Though the faubourgs were destroyed, the city within was not, and it still remains very much as it used to be. Its streets are so narrow that there is barely room for a carriage to go through them. In many of them there is not room, and therefore carriages are very little used in "la vieille cité," as it is called. In the old time they went on horseback or on foot.

In this ancient place are some of the most remarkable buildings in all France. By far the most remarkable is the cathedral, which is simply a gem of architecture. There are few churches that resemble it at all, because of its peculiar and wonderfully harmonious combination of widely different kinds of building. The nave is ancient Romanesque with columns alternately round and square — a rare combination indeed. The square columns have four semi-detached round columns, one on each side, which support the vaulting of the roof. The transepts and apse are Gothic of the most perfect style of the fourteenth century. The capitals of the columns are most exquisitely carved, and the many statues which adorn these columns, about midway in their height, are cut from the solid stone and not attached as is usually the case. They are wonderful works of art, full of the dignity and the intense devotional spirit so truly characteristic of the Gothic work of that time.

Then there is the glory of the stained glass, magnificent in color and design. The two rose windows are hardly to be surpassed anywhere, and the lofty windows about the apse and in the side chapels are also very beautiful. That familiar subject, "The Tree of Jesse," occupies one of these windows, but the treatment of it has none of that comical element which was so irresistible in the church at Beauvais. On the contrary, it is exquisitely beautiful. The abundant foliage of the tree is interwoven with the whole design, and the figures of the kings and prophets seem to be embowered among the green leaves. There is another window equally beautiful, of which the central pane of the design is the Crucifixion. But not even with such a subject does the artist permit his figures to interfere at all with his thought of color.

The church, fascinating as it is, is not the most remarkable part of Carcassonne — neither is the château, which is also within the walls. One cannot linger to look at the ruins of the cloisters and the bishop's palace that once were here, because the tour of the ramparts is by far the most interesting sight in this place of marvels.

To go around the ramparts of Carcassonne is not an easy thing to do. It means a walk of at least a mile, beside going up and down steep flights of stairs almost every other minute. There is also some of the excitement which comes from actual danger, for if the mistral is blowing as it was on the day when I went round the ramparts, it is not so easy to keep your footing on the narrow "courtines" that are just behind the crenellated wall. There is no railing, no protection at all, and if one should make a misstep the consequences would be serious enough.

But even if there is a little danger about it when the mistral is at its full force, no one would wish to miss the tour of the ramparts of Carcassonne, because here, as perhaps nowhere else in the world, can mediæval warfare, and mediæval life also, be studied and understood.

There are at Carcassonne two distinct lines of defence — the outer "enceinte," as it is called, and the inner. Beyond the outer one was the moat, also a most important part of the defences of the fortress. These two walls, which surround the town at different heights, — the outer one being very much lower than the inner, — are surmounted by fifty-four towers of the most solid masonry, so disposed as to protect one another in the most perfect way known to the

military science of those days. It is an object-
lesson, and many who pride themselves on their
knowledge of history could learn from this place
in much the same way as a child learns in a kin-
dergarten. It is one thing to read about sieges in
mediæval times. It is quite another almost to see
one carried on before your very eyes.

At one point on the ramparts near the château,
which is within the walls, can be seen another defence, the barbican, which is far down in the valley
below, and connected with the walls by a fortified
passage, which abruptly climbs the steep hill. The
barbican itself, which was a very strong round tower,
has disappeared, and a church has taken its place,
but the whole disposition of it and its means of
access to the fortress above can easily be discerned.
It was in itself a place of great strength, and yet
if it were taken hardly anything would be accom-
plished toward the subjugation of Carcassonne.

There was another barbican on the other side to
defend the gate over there — but it is not possible
to describe all the elaborate defences of this most
extraordinary fortress without writing a scientific
treatise upon it, as did the famous architect who
restored these walls and towers, M. Viollet-le-Duc.

Those who wish accurate and technical information about this old town must have recourse to his

brochure, " La Cité Carcassonne," for they will find nowhere else such valuable information upon this fascinating though most intricate subject.

But even those who have not studied deeply into these matters are perforce put into mediæval times in making the tour of Carcassonne's walls. The towers by the gates have still the grooves in which the portcullises were worked up and down. By each of these grooves is an opening about a foot and a half wide in the second story of the tower and as long as the width of the portcullis itself, through which all manner of projectiles could be discharged upon the heads of the unfortunate soldiers attempting to assail the closed portcullis below. In these towers by the gates are places to store the great round stones that were hurled down, and immense fireplaces where the oil could be heated that was even more deadly in effect than the huge stones when it was poured boiling hot from this height on the attacking force.

There is one tower on the walls of Carcassonne whose heating arrangements had a very different purpose from that of boiling oil. This is the tower of the Inquisition — an enormous tower. In its upper story still exists the immense fireplace where the irons of torture were heated. Here the judges sat and interrogated those to whom the hot irons were applied. If they remained obdurate, there were several stories below where other means could be used to induce them to embrace the gentle faith of the inquisitor. Lowest of all there is a story which can now be reached only by a ladder — perhaps it was so then — and here is a post to which are attached chains. When this was discovered not very many years ago, human bones were found among the many links of these long chains which held the victim till he died. This tower is too terrible to linger in. It makes one shudder even to look at it, especially because it is not fully restored within, and its immense depth yawns far below like some terrible abyss into which human souls might be plunged. It is like a passage from Dante's "Inferno."

But there are other towers whose uses were not so horrible. There is the Tour du Moulin — a most majestic structure. In this the bread was prepared for the garrison. It had a windmill once that rose from its roof — hence its name — but this has disappeared. Enough remains, however, to show how the food was prepared, and in what curious, half-open ovens the bread was baked.

Water was, of course, essential in a beleaguered town, and there were several deep wells at Carcassonne, one so deep that it is said the bottom has not been found; another quite deep enough is now partially filled up.

Then there was the Tower of Justice. Did they have justice in those days? The walls of this tower were formerly hung with tapestry, and the iron hooks still remain from which the tapestries depended. There is the private entrance for the judges, which must have been behind the tapestries, and a public entrance for every one else, that opens upon the ramparts. If the records of this court in the tower had been kept, what secrets they might have disclosed! But they are lost.

And then there is the Bishop's tower. He needed apparently to be fortified more than anybody else, for his tower is "on horseback" over the outer and inner lines of fortification, the only one that has so commanding a position. Clearly he did not put all his faith in the power of the spiritual arm, but required a most advantageous position for his men-at-arms. This tower would enable him to isolate his own precinct from all the rest of the fortress, and make it a fort within a fort which would have to be separately attacked after all the rest had been taken. But he must not be blamed for this, because the lords of the château did the same thing. All else in Carcassonne might be taken and their castle still remain an almost unassailable stronghold.

Truly it is a marvellous place. The imagination is tempted to run riot here, because what is actually seen hardly seems real, for the reason that it is so unaccustomed to our thought; and what is told hardly seems real either, because we understand so little about the gentle and gracious customs and habits of Simon de Montfort or inquisitors like those of the grewsome tower.

Without some touch of enthusiasm, some play of fancy, it is not possible to get into the spirit of Carcassonne. It has been described analytically by Henry James. It has been described scientifically by M. Viollet-le-Duc. The latter has done more than describe it. He has rebuilt it and made it possible to repeople it in thought. This he did not attempt to do, but many a writer, many a poet, will find in his work the scene for story, drama, or poem that has to do with days long past.

The spirit of the place can hardly be better illustrated to-day than by telling of the effect produced by seeing a regiment of French dragoons pass along beneath the walls. In this magnificent army of the French is power enough to destroy every wall and tower of Carcassonne in one day, and yet these dragoons seem out of place. The ancient walls, the tremendous towers, look sternly upon them. They fear them not because they do not know them.

In the days of their pride, knights came up these steep ascents, clad in bright armor, with waving plumes upon their helmets. Their squires and all their retinue followed, and lances were carried high and pennants fluttered in the breeze.

There were heralds to bespeak the warders of the towers, and all was stately and impressive. If battle came it was a contest of man to man, of wall and tower against mine and ram and beleaguering trenches. If the drawbridge was let down and the double portcullises raised that the knights and their following might enter, then afterward came the tournament in the lists between the outer and the inner "enceinte," and the reward of martial prowess and of ladies' favors was to be won.

To one who has yielded to the dream of Carcassonne, the presence of the dragoons seems like an impertinence, and yet, sad as the waking from that dream is, the thought that these once impregnable walls and towers are but as card houses before the power of the armies of to-day is even more sad because it means the weakness of what once was strong.

CHAPTER IX

TRAVELLING in the south of France is not always a pleasant thing, especially in the month of March when the mistral is at its worst. Perhaps it is be-cause of the discomforts that must be endured here that so little seems to be known among us about places that are not only most interesting in them-selves, but simply brimming over with so many sug-gestions about times past that it is difficult to tell which to choose and lay special emphasis upon, where all is so full of interest to any one who cares to study French history.

Aigues-Mortes is about an hour and a half by rail from Nîmes; but this does not mean by an express train. On the contrary, there are stops every five minutes, and really the laziness of the people seems to have penetrated the locomotive. The country is flat and uninteresting, and as one nears Aigues-Mortes it becomes worse than uninteresting. Here it is des-olate and repellant. Immense salt marshes stretch far away on either hand, and there are stagnant waters, most unpleasantly suggestive of malaria.

Nevertheless, the natives seem to think that one ought to have a good appetite, for when I asked for some sandwiches for luncheon they gave me a very remarkable combination of bread and ham: it must have been at least three inches thick. A giant's mouth could scarcely compass it, and even the giant with a digestion proportionate to his size would be sorry if he had succeeded in the attempt, because of the heaviness of the bread and the toughness of the ham. Nevertheless, it was that or nothing, and, dividing our sandwiches into various parts, we did as well as we could.

I was glad afterward that we struggled with the sandwiches, for eating or drinking at Aigues-Mortes is not so agreeable as it might be. The town is so dirty that one hesitates before touching anything in it. It is full of malaria. The stagnant waters are the cause of this. The people are so yellow that it seems as if they were all afflicted with jaundice.

Fortunately, it is not necessary to stay here over night. One can leave Nîmes in the morning and return in time for dinner, after seeing all that is really of great interest in the place. What is to be seen, however, is of such importance that all discomforts are soon forgotten.

AIGUES-MORTES

The historical interest centres about Louis IX., —
St. Louis, — though later there is much in the history
of the place that is well worth knowing. It was
from here that Louis IX. embarked twice. In 1248
he went hence with a great army and eight hundred
galleys to Egypt. He took his queen, Marguerite,
with him. In that expedition he was successful; but
in 1270 he embarked again from Aigues-Mortes to
attack the infidels at Tunis. This was fatal to him.
In less than a month after he started he was dead.

It is hard to see how Louis IX. could have got
his army to the sea from this place, because it is no
port at all, but simply surrounded by marshes. There
is a story that he made a canal which gave entrance
to a bay quite a distance away. The canal does not
exist now, but possibly it once was there. At all
events, it is certain that the king did embark here,
and the Porte de la Marine is shown as the place
where his soldiers entered the ships.

Coming to quite a different period of history, it
is also certain that Francis I. of France, and
Charles V. of Spain met here. The house where
they met is still pointed out as one of the principal sights of the place. It is not far from
Louis IX.'s Porte de la Marine, and is on the
" Boulevard François Premier." Observe the pride
of the French. Here is a boulevard in a town

which is not big enough to have a street, and really has not any worthy of the name.

But all this is merely a preface to Aigues-Mortes. The interest of the place to-day comes from what it is, and the wonder of it comes from the fact that it still is what it was. After Carcassonne it would hardly seem possible that another walled town would be interesting, and yet it is true that Aigues-Mortes is even more interesting than Carcassonne in some ways, for the simple reason that it is more perfectly preserved. There is much restoration at Carcassonne — there is hardly any at Aigues-Mortes. This walled town of Louis IX. and Philip the Bold remains almost exactly as they left it. The force of the mistral has had some influence upon it; for there are many places where this terrible wind seems to have literally dug into the stones, but it could not penetrate far enough to materially impair their solidity and strength.

The sieges it underwent seem to have had little effect upon it, although the face of one tower is full of small holes made by the projectiles of the Burgundians, who had taken the town by storming a gate, but were utterly foiled in their efforts to take the ramparts and towers. These little holes on the face of the massive stones show how ludicrously impotent the force of attacking weapons was in those days against such walls as these. They had little more effect than a child's pop-gun.

Aigues-Mortes to-day is, as it used to be, a mediæval city surrounded by lofty walls with cre-nellated ramparts, from which rise fifteen massive towers, and through which penetrate nine strongly fortified gates. There is not here, as at Carcassonne, a double line of ramparts, nor has the place the advantage of a high hill to assist in its defence. It had, however, once an immense moat, which the surrounding waters made it easy to keep full; but this has entirely disappeared, because the stagnant water in it so aggravated the malaria of the place, already bad enough, that it became necessary to fill it up.

Of all the towers on these old walls the most interesting is the Tour de Constance. This is one of the most immense and impressive of all the mediæval towers of Europe. It is far larger than any tower at Carcassonne. Its walls are at least fifteen feet thick, and its diameter inside these walls is sixty-five feet. The height is ninety feet, and above the flat space of its roof rises a small tower, used formerly as a lighthouse. This small tower is thirty-four feet in height, making the total height one hundred and twenty-four feet.

St. Louis made this upper tower and he used it
as a beacon. There is an iron cap on its summit
in which bonfires could be made to serve as
signals. The iron of which this cap is made was
taken by St. Louis from a tower built by Charlemagne on another part of the walls. It is, therefore, more than one thousand years old and remains
quite as good as ever it was.

From the top of this beacon tower the whole
of Aigues-Mortes can easily be studied. It lies at
your feet. Every tower, every gate, the whole
round of the ramparts, the low houses with their
tiled roofs, the churches, the narrow streets — all
is spread out before you as if it were drawn upon
a map. It is a fascinating sight. It is not only
what you see, but what you think. This is not
the home of the few poor, squalid people that
appear at rare intervals on the streets. It is the
home of those who have long passed away but to
the mind seem still to be here.

It is hard to say which is the more interesting, —
the view from the top of this tower, or what is to be
seen within it. There are four stories, the lower one
being a place of storage for provisions, to which access was had by openings in the floor of each of the
stories above, that were provided with ropes and
buckets for bringing up the grain from below. There

was also a deep well with similar appliances for providing each story with water. The architecture is very early Gothic, exceedingly pure and fine in style, and admirably preserved. The first and second stories seem like immense chapels of some vast Gothic cathedral.

Each story has its means of defence, as though it were intended to be a separate fortress. The winding stone stairway, that leads from one to the other, is most curiously defended at every point by angular projections of stone, behind which the soldiers could be sheltered while they shot at those attempting to ascend the stairs.

But all this story of battle and bloodshed does not exhaust the interest of the Tour de Constance. There is beside all this a most pathetic history that must be told about it, for here in the upper one of the two great rooms were imprisoned for years many who refused to abjure their religion after the revocation of the Edict of Nantes. A number of these poor prisoners were women. Some have written their names upon the merciless stones, using, as it is said, their finger nails to make the letters. Sometimes they used their knitting-needles. Many and many a name can be read upon these walls — some of them of the noblest families of France. Here in this vaulted room with its impenetrable walls, these poor

G

creatures, strong only in their love of the right, lingered year after year, and when they died, as most of them did, their bodies were probably thrown into the salt marshes, and they were forgotten.

The eloquence of these speechless stones in this mediæval fortress of France is marvellous. It is extraordinary how the stones do tell stories. Though Jacques, the melancholy, says there are sermons in them, he does not by any means exhaust the subject. Some stones can instruct as well as preach, and the stones of Aigues-Mortes are simply professors of history.

For instance, there is a great stone in this upper room where these poor captives lingered that has its particular story to tell. It is like a millstone, and to-day it is lying on the floor of the room where so many life histories were ended so far as this world is concerned. What was it intended for? It was used to grind the grain that was brought up in the buckets from the reservoir three stories below. Thus were the poor prisoners fed. There was a great open fireplace, and there, when the grain was ground, they made their cakes and baked them before the fire; and they quenched their thirst from the rain-water caught on the platform above, and falling thence to the cistern, whence it was lifted to them just as was the unground grain.

The picture is so vivid, so intense in its reality, that it truly seems most strange not to see the captives themselves here. Why should all their surroundings remain perfect in every detail, and all the human life be gone that once filled the place?

There is still another side to the picture of Aigues-Mortes. Why has the human life gone out of the streets as well as the tower? There was a time when these were crowded with knights in armor, and on every shield was a cross. There were crosses on the banners — there were crosses everywhere, and in the name of that sacred symbol the knights went hence on the last of the crusades. It was a daring — a most hazardous deed. They must brave the storms of the Mediterranean, fearfully severe at times, and they must meet the Saracens, an enemy by no means to be despised. The knights are gone, and few now walk the streets they once thronged.

When St. Louis directed his hosts toward the ships that were to take them through the canal to the sea, I hope he did not look as he looks to-day in the statue of him made by Pradier. This is in the principal, in fact, the only square of Aigues-Mortes. It is of bronze and is heroic in size. The statue is quite unworthy of so noble a subject. It would be easy to ridicule it, but this is not well, for it had a serious intention, and the people of Aigues-Mortes are extremely proud of it. There are many photographs of it and many, too, of the walls and towers, but the photograph cannot give the real picture of Aigues-Mortes.

History must paint that picture. It was the scene of the embarkation. The churches were full of those who came to the mass, and left their offerings that prayers might be said for their souls if they died. When the religious rites were finished, all went to the great Porte de la Marine and men and horses were put upon the ships to start upon their perilous, though glorious, voyage. Each face is lighted by religious and martial enthusiasm. The good king turns to bless his land, which he was never to see again. The walls of Aigues-Mortes fade in the distance.

When St. Louis with all his army has left the place because inspired by faith and religious fervor, it would be well for us to leave it too. It is better to go away from such a fortress with a thought of the highest that was in the spirit of it, and to forget if possible what was cruel and barbarous.

CHAPTER X

CUSTODIANS OF FRENCH CHURCHES AND MONUMENTS

THE custodians of the French churches and monuments are very interesting people. I have often wished I could have had more time to talk with them, and find out how they came to be where they are, and how they learned what they know about their buildings.

There is an old man at St. Ouen whose face should be painted by some tenderly sympathetic artist. There is an expression in it which seems to come in some way from the very church itself. There is the same placidity, the same nobility of line, and there is the same kind of love that those who made the windows must have felt. This custodian is not the "Swiss" to whom I have before referred. This one is too old to mount the stairs and only shows to visitors the lower part of the church.

Taking visitors about St. Ouen is not a task to him. Although he does it many times a day, he loves it more each time.

"Now, gentlemen and ladies, will you be kind enough to step here for just one moment? If you love Gothic architecture, I think I can show you the most beautiful Gothic view in the world. No — not there — a little farther this way, if you please. I want you to see the columns with all their lines and forms, and at the same time the stained glass. There! That's right! There's where Mr. Ruskin used to stand. Did you ever see anything so beautiful as that? I have been in this church for more than thirty years, and I find new beauties in it every day. Have you seen the reflection in the vessel that contains the holy water? No! Well, then, you must see it, because it will give you a better idea of the lines of the church than anything else. Have you been above to go about the clerestory under the arches just by the painted windows? Oh! you must certainly go there. You cannot understand the church at all unless you see it from that point, and it is necessary to know all about St. Ouen, because if you do not you will miss one of the very loveliest things in the world. I wish I could go up with you, but I am too old. My brother here will do that. I will stay here and wait to hear what you think. I love to wait in the church. Please tell me whether you think it is beautiful."

And so the old man waited as he doubtless waited every day for other visitors. I hope that many give to his dearly loved church that enthusiastic praise which delights him. Praise of St. Ouen is to him like food and drink. He lifts up his head when he hears it, and he walks proudly. He points again to the columns and the windows. He also forgets his fee, — at least he does not ask for it. When it is given without his asking, he takes it, and looks pleased, but immediately begins again his talk about the church. He hopes you will stay just a little longer. "There is one beautiful point of view on the other side. You have not seen that yet."

This custodian of St. Ouen was one of the most benignant-looking men I ever saw, and in his language he was one of the most enthusiastic. He surely must have been an intelligent Christian gentleman.

There was a custodian at Falaise who interested me greatly. He did not seem so much in love with his subject as was the one at St. Ouen, or at Aigues-Mortes. However, seeing my interest in the place, he began to warm up a little after a while. He was quite an old man — between sixty and seventy, I should think, and I began to talk to him about his life, because I thought he had a peculiar history. He looked like a disappointed man. There was something almost like a tragedy written on his face.

"How long have you been here?" I said.

"Oh! not very long," was the reply.

"Well, what did you do before you came here?"

"Ah! Monsieur, I was at Mont St. Michel."

This then was the tragedy — here was the disappointment of a lifetime, to be no longer at Mont St. Michel.

"Monsieur, are you going to Mont St. Michel?"

"Yes, I am going there."

"You will find everything of beauty in the universe there. There is no other place like that. Alas! that I am too old to mount its stairs and go about it as once I did."

"But Falaise is very interesting. It is one of the finest Norman castles in France."

"Oh! yes, it is interesting — certainly it is very fine — but there is only one Mont St. Michel."

The custodian of Aigues-Mortes was, I think, the only lively person I saw in the place. The atmosphere is not wholesome, and most of the people (there are not many) look sickly and have a most dejected air. It seems to be an effort for them to move about at all.

But this custodian loved the walls and towers of Aigues-Mortes just as that one at Carcassonne loved his, or the one at St. Ouen his church.

If I could write down all he said, I would have directly a book too bulky for publication. It was not possible to stop for a minute the flow of his — not conversation, but monologue. Every detail about the place, especially in the Tour de Constance, was given with a volubility peculiarly French, and an accuracy of knowledge quite French also. There was not a king or queen who had ever been at Aigues-Mortes with whom he was not acquainted, and as to the prisoners in the tower, I think they must all have been his personal friends. He knew how and where they ate and drank and slept, and the minutest details of their way of living.

I had often wondered whether there was a college somewhere in France where these custodians were educated, and whether they had to be graduated and receive their diplomas before they could get a position in one of the historical monuments. In talking with one of the custodians at Fontainebleau, I found that such was not the case. The custodians study the history of a building from the archives kept in it or in the library of the town.

CHAPTER XI

FAR up among the Pyrenees in a green valley walled in by high cliffs and towering snow-clad mountains, nestles the little town of St. Sauveur. The magnificent scenery about it is its greatest charm, but often this cannot be seen on account of the low-hanging rain-clouds. There are, however, other things that can be seen here even if it does rain. Of these the most interesting is the Church of the Templars at Luz. The walk from St. Sauveur to Luz is not a long one, — only about a mile, — but it is so very lovely that one wishes it were a great deal longer.

At first it seems strange that these religious warriors who had risked life itself in the effort to conquer and retain Jerusalem, and had succeeded in their attempt even to the point of holding their conquest for a while, should have built this little church in a Pyrenean valley. The reason, however, is not hard to find. When they could no longer hold the

THE CHURCH OF THE TEMPLARS AT LUZ

Holy Land, they had to come back to defend their own country against the Saracens who had now, in their turn, become invaders. Luz is near the Spanish frontier, and commands a pass leading into Spain. Therefore, the Templars built their fortress-church here, and, for the same reason, long afterwards it was used as a defence against the Spaniards.

No other church of the Knights Templar that I have ever seen is so well preserved as this. It is thought by some writers to be almost unique.

Its history is bewildering because it was used for so many different purposes in the centuries since it was founded, but its architecture is no less bewildering. Here are combined two characteristic qualities of the very early Romanesque, — the military use of it, and the way it was used in churches.

There are ramparts about this church, distant from it about forty feet. In one part of the space between the two was the cemetery where the Knights Templar were buried, and their bones are still there. I have never seen so many human bones together in any other place unless it be the church of the Capuchins at Rome. It is hard to help stumbling over them in walking about between the church and the ramparts.

> " Their bones are dust,
> Their good swords, rust,
> Their souls are with the saints, we trust."

To an architect the chief interest of the building would be in its principal portal, for this is one of the most remarkable examples I have ever seen of the earliest Romanesque. It dates from the tenth century, I think, at least a part of it does. Some of the wall of the church near by it has been restored. It somewhat resembles the portal of Morlaas church, but has not the very curious figures that make that so interesting. There are six concentric arches, recessed one behind the other, giving a very massive and imposing character to the entrance, although it is not really very large. A bas-relief of Christ and the four evangelists directly over the low door, and under the lowest arch, is a most curious specimen of that rude sculpture which the earliest Romanesque builders were fond of using wherever they could find a place to put it in. All the decorations of the arches are most unusual. In one the pattern is an arabesque distinctly Moorish in character. Perhaps the Templars found this in their adventurous journeys to the far east, or they may have borrowed it from Spain. The capitals of the columns that support each arch are also curious. They differ in their carved ornamentation. All are somewhat crude in execution, but whatever their faults may be they have a certain dignity and expressiveness quite worthy of their position at the entrance of the sacred building.

This interesting portal is very different from that by which the poor " Cagots " were allowed to enter to reach a separate chapel reserved for their use. That was a low door in the ramparts through which they must have crawled on hands and knees and beyond it a very small door by which they could reach their chapel. It would be interesting to trace the history of these " Cagots." There are many traditions about them. Some say they embraced the Arian heresy; others that they were a separate race of people descended perhaps from the Moors, perhaps from the lost tribes of Israel. Certain it is that they were treated very much as lepers are. No one would have anything to do with them, and their very name expresses contempt and abhorrence.

It was an act of unusual tolerance in those days to allow these proscribed people to worship so near the faithful, but it does seem strange that those who wished to worship the same God in a Christian church should be separated by such impassable barriers from the other worshippers.

In the principal church there is another kind of separation in the worship; that is, the men have their place in the upper part of the building and the women below. The larger part of the nave has two stories, both open toward the altar. The women worshipped on the stone floor of the church below; the men in the wooden gallery attached to the great columns that support the roof at a point about midway in the height of the nave itself. It was a most effectual separation truly; for neither could see the other, and to hear a word whispered or even spoken would be difficult, perhaps impossible. It is a wonder that neither the Puritans nor the Quakers ever thought of such an arrangement. Perhaps it may be because the history of the Templars shows that not even such strict regulations as these were always successful in attaining their object.

It would not be possible to describe all the curious things in this most remarkable church, — it would need a book to do that; but the museum must not be omitted. It is a very small room indeed, reached by a narrow flight of steps, and was probably connected at one time with the church. Possibly it may have been the abode of the Prior-Commander of the Templar Knights. Small as it is, it contains more relics of the Templars than any other place I ever saw. There are bits for their war-horses of such size and cruel form that it is no wonder these famous horsemen could control their steeds as they pleased. The only wonder is they did not break their jaws with a leverage of nearly a foot on a curb of heavy, closely joined steel rings. Their spurs, of which there are several here, are not so formidable, although quite strong enough. Their swords and lances are here, and the pikes and small arms of their attendants. Then there are many curious things which they must have brought back with them from the East; among them an alabaster image of the Virgin and Child, which is quite archaic in style, and must be very ancient. There is a picture of the Trinity, which is the most curious representation on canvas of that most difficult subject to paint successfully that I have ever seen or heard of. At the top of the picture are three foreheads, three noses, three mouths, three chins, four cheeks and four eyes, joined together in one monstrous head, which is not attached to a body but placed above a triangle on the sides of which are written "Filius non est — Pater non est — Spiritus non est," all the uncompleted sentences being led by white lines to the word "Deus" in the centre. This word is supposed to be the heart of the body, of which the combination of noses, chins, cheeks, and eyes is the head. Such a picture is almost unique. It would be the most prized gem of many a collector of ancient works of art — but it is clear up here among the Pyrenees, and money cannot get it away because this Templar church is a French "historical monument" and nothing in it is for sale on any terms. High prices have often been offered for many things in this little room, but they have always been refused.

If one wishes to come close to the very life and spirit of the Templar monks, he must go to Luz. It is easy to read about them, but here one can see them just as he can a siege at Carcassonne.

CHAPTER XII

POITIERS is nearly a city of churches. The battlefield is not far away, but there is little of interest to see there now. These churches are so remarkable, that the ecclesiastical architecture of France in its historical development can only be partially understood without studying them. The most noted of the churches are the " Temple de St. Jean," the church of "Notre Dame de Poitiers," and the cathedral. I name them in the order of age. The first is thought by some who have studied deeply into these subjects, to be the oldest Christian church in France. The date of its foundation is not accurately known. Some say the sixth or seventh century ; others claim that parts of it are as old as the third or fourth.

If any one knows, it must be the learned Belgian, Professor Delaroche whom I met there, hard at work, as he has been for the last five years, writing a history of it. If a man who has achieved such a success that he is now a member of twenty-nine societies of

learning in Europe, finds it worth his while to give
so large a part of his life to this one building, it
must indeed be remarkable.*

He fixes a much earlier date than the sixth century for its foundation, and believes that it was
begun not later than the fourth. This church was
originally a baptistery. The font, large and deep
enough for immersion, still remains, and also the
pipes to bring the water in, and to carry it off. The
architecture and the masonry show something of the
Roman manner, and something of the Visigothic.
There is little beauty about it. It is small, even
with the additions of porch and apse which were
made to convert the baptistery into a church. There
are no columns and aisles and painted windows to
make it charming to the eye—but it is most interesting to stand within what may have been the first
Christian church in France.

The venerable temple is now a museum, filled with
most curious carvings and fragments of buildings
found in the neighborhood, and there are also several
sarcophagi of the Merovingian period, which were
discovered near by not many years ago.

The church of Notre Dame de Poitiers is perfectly
fascinating. The Romanesque façade is carved with
sculpture from base to tower top. The effect is indescribably rich. Surely Haig's attention has not

NOTRE DAME DE POITIERS

been called to this marvel of florid Romanesque or he would have etched it long ago. It is one of the few profusely sculptured façades in France which retain nearly all the figures uninjured except by the touch of time. Apostles, martyrs, kings, and prophets, Adam and Eve, and all the patriarchs, many a Bible story, many from lives of saints, are sculptured here with most delightful confusion and irrelevance of subject, but with most perfect and delicious artistic harmony of line and form. There is a porch at the side, too, whose rounded Roman arch is nearly as richly sculptured.

There are two circular turrets that flank the gable of the façade, and these are as picturesque as anything else in the beautiful old building.

The whole of it is wondrously mellowed by long exposure to sun, and rain, and wind. There is a glow about it like that of a very old picture. The outlines of the innumerable figures are softened. Not one angle remains.

This ancient church, with all its magnificent wealth of ornament, stands modestly in the market-place, and the booths of the peasants are about it. The common people come and go with their fruits and flowers and vegetables, and there are busy noisy little carts and quaint old vehicles that seem nearly as ancient as the church itself.

Within they have tried to make the old church vain by covering her arches and vaulted roofs with hideous, glaring, modern painting, supposed to be a restoration, but in reality a murder of all the interior beauty. If it had been let alone, it would have been charming. As it is, after a single glance one seeks the door, and leaves it with a shudder.

The cathedral of St. Pierre, founded by Henry II. of England, is quite as remarkable as Notre Dame de Poitiers, though in a very different way. Here the interior is the chief charm. It is one of the noblest specimens of Poitevine architecture in existence. The simplicity, harmony, grace, and strength of its lines and construction are admirable in the highest degree. This peculiar style combines the round arch of the Romanesque with the pointed of the Gothic in a most peculiar and beautiful way. No dissonance is perceived between them. On the contrary, one melts into the other with some curious sympathy of grace. There are other most interesting churches in Poitiers, especially St. Radegonde, and there are many quaint buildings with richly carved façades. Perhaps the most remarkable of these is the house of Diane de Poitiers, where she lived long with her husband, Louis de Brézé, Grand Seneschal of Normandy, before she went to the French court and captivated Henry II.

The battle-field of Poitiers is naturally interesting to all English-speaking people, but it is difficult to locate it exactly now. The French have not been careful to preserve the monuments of their most disastrous defeat. Moreover, a railroad has traversed the field where the French king was taken and the Black Prince destroyed the flower of the French chivalry. The configuration of the country is not, however, greatly changed, and it is still possible to see what an advantage the English soldier had in his admirably chosen position, while the French had to advance up a slope with the sun in their eyes. But all this is a matter of history. I only wished in this chapter to emphasize the beauty of the churches of Poitiers, for it seems that but few Americans come to the lovely old town.

CHAPTER XIII

TWO ANCIENT BÉARNAIS CHURCHES

THE cathedral of Lescar — for it was a cathedral once — is not far from Pau. In about three-quarters of an hour one can drive there. The place is hardly less interesting historically than Pau itself, for Lescar was once the seat of government of the Béarnais region which afterward was merged in the kingdom of Navarre.

It is upon the crest of one of those low hills about Pau which are wonderful because of the views they command of the fertile valley, the "coteaux" with their trees and vines, and the snow-clad Pyrenees rising beyond.

There was a castle at Lescar which long antedated the château at Pau. Gaston Phœbus was not born when this castle was built, nor was many a prince of his line before him. There is very little left of it now, only a ruined tower, a most picturesque arched gateway, and a bit of wall here and there. What is left artists would love to paint, but in the church itself architects would delight more than painters, because here is one of the few remaining specimens of the very old Norman architecture. According to proper definition, it is not Norman at all. Some of those who describe it call it Romanesque, but it is not exactly that either. I call it Norman because we are more accustomed to associate with that word than any other, heavy, round arches, and massive columns and a simple ornament about the capitals of the columns not in the least like the carvings of the Gothic architects.

The façade of this church might well have excited the interest even of a Richardson; for some of his arched doorways are made upon nearly the same lines as this one, but he uses much more ornament. There is something most interesting about these deeply recessed openings into a church. In the mind of the builder it must have been clear that one should come gradually from the full light of day into the softened light of the sanctuary. He must also have felt that there should be a thought of humility in entering a place of worship, for the concentred arches become smaller and smaller as the entrance is reached.

But the chief interest of the cathedral of Lescar is not in this façade, simple and yet imposing as it is. The columns inside are the most remarkable things about the church, and these are interesting in many ways. Their bases are great round masses of stone, far larger than the columns that surmount them — so much larger that they seem rather unnecessary for the support of the somewhat low roof which they uphold. Possibly they were stronger than what was really needed, but the architect of those days preferred stability to anything else. He wished his building to stand for all time if possible. This building *has* stood for more than a thousand years, and even now it shows few signs of old age.

This architecture is so massive in form, so stern in line, that it seems hardly possible it could have been splendidly decorated, and yet such is the fact. At least all of the apse in this church was covered with frescoes. Nor were they bad pictures either, when one thinks how long ago they were painted. There is something in the spirit of them strongly suggestive of Giotto. Nobody knows who painted them, but it is not impossible that some Italian artist of the early days of Italian art had a hand in it; for they may have been painted much later than the time of the building of the church.

There are wonderful wood-carvings about the altar stalls here, quaint in style but very direct and powerful in expression. But to the student the most interesting carvings in the church would

be those about the capitals of the columns. I do
not know the history of them, but it is certain that
they are truly in the very spirit of that early architecture of which so few specimens remain. The
familiar "dog's tooth" and "saw-edge" way of
ornamenting is to be seen all through this church,
but I think I have never seen dragons or devils
used with such immense effect in an ornamental
way.

On several columns there are double dragons —
twins they might be, like the Siamese — united at
only one point, but actuated by a common desire of
devouring sinners. Each mouth has a bad man's
head in it, and each tail is coiled about a bad
man's legs. I only know they are bad because
otherwise they would not have been thus treated.
The expressions of their faces do not indicate
suffering or alarm — rather idiocy or stupefaction.
This is very amusing, but the most interesting
thing to a student of art is that these extraordinary
figures are really decorative and made to harmonize
in line and form with the columns whose capitals
they decorate. I should have expected this in
Gothic, but not in early Romanesque. For this
reason among others I think this church one of
the most remarkable examples of that rare style
to be found anywhere.

This study of the Lescar cathedral leads naturally
to a thought of the other one at Morlaas, and not
only because of some relation between the architecture of the two, but also on account of a certain
resemblance between them in their history. The
cathedral of Lescar was built in expiation for a
murder. The church at Morlaas also owes its existence to what the priests callèd a crime, but it was
one of quite a different kind. Centulle was the
criminal, and yet he seems to have been one of the
very best kings Béarn ever had. He helped the poor,
lightened the taxes, improved the roads, modified the
severity of the laws, and promoted justice as far as
he could; but, unfortunately, he fell in love with
Gisla, who was too nearly related to him for marriage to be possible under the canons of the Roman
Church. He married her, nevertheless, and from their
union came that Gaston whose descendants were to
be such illustrious princes at Pau, and one of whom,
Gaston Phœbus, was to found the château there.

Pope Gregory VII. heard of this marriage, and
wrote a letter to Centulle, telling him he must put
away his wife, Gisla, and expiate his crime by devot-
ing himself to the church. He did so, and because
of that command of the Pope, the church at Morlaas
was built, and most richly endowed. It is the story
of the Abbaye aux Hommes and the Abbaye aux

Dames over again, though William and Matilda do not seem to have obeyed the Pope's mandate in quite the same way as did Centulle and Gisla.

The story of Gisla's after life, when her husband had been taken from her by the papal mandate, is one of the most interesting chapters in mediæval history. This noble woman, whose love — whose all that made life sweet — had been torn from her, did not lose her faith or her courage. She resolved to found a retreat for gentlewomen who had determined to give up the world; not exactly a nunnery, but even stricter in its rules than those of the nuns. She built a building at Marcigny, in the region of the Loire. Here she dwelt herself, and others who had been afflicted in a similar way also dwelt there with her. Those who came there came to stay until death took them away, and they were never to go outside the walls until death called them. There came a fire in the town one day, and this retreat seemed doomed. Hugues, the venerable Archbishop of Lyons, was there, and he absolved the women from their vows and commanded them to come out. Gisla said it would be better to pray that the fire might be extinguished, and said it mattered little how those within the threatened walls met death, because they were there to await it. The archbishop then did pray that the flames might be stayed, and they were; but not one of the noble women left those walls before death, if history tells the truth.

This was Gisla's part of the sacrifice required by the Pope. Centulle married again, but he never ceased to care for the Church of the Holy Faith at Morlaas, which he founded because of his sin, and it became a very rich and most important church in those days.

There is not very much left of the old part of the church of Morlaas now, but there is enough to show that it was and is one of the most remarkable examples of very ancient Romanesque in all this region. The façade is the most interesting part of the building, because it shows exactly what were the entrances to churches in the early Romanesque time, and how they were related in style to the magnificent Gothic portals that followed them many years afterward. There are points of close resemblance most interesting to trace, and there are the widest differences.

The great central arch of the Morlaas façade and the arches on each side of it are altogether Romanesque and very richly ornamented. Above the central arch the architecture is distinctly Gothic of a very early period. There is the pointed form, with pinnacles and gargoyles, and there is an unmistakable suggestion of the buttress construction, so characteristic of the Gothic, though not in its fully developed form.

THE CHURCH OF THE HOLY FAITH AT MORLAAS

A very curious thing about this upper part of the
façade is the way the three bells are placed in it.   Instead of being in a belfry or tower they are in open
niches in the wall itself.   The clock is placed in the
centre — one bell over it and one on each side.   The
effect is most peculiar.   I do not remember seeing
such an arrangement anywhere else.   I was not able
to find out just when this Gothic addition was made.
Perhaps the date is not known, for a very old history
of the church which I consulted says nothing of it.

There is doubt also about the real meaning of the
figures, which are arranged in concentric semicircles
upon the arches that together form the great recessed doorway.   In the old history I spoke of, written before the restorations were made, some meanings
were suggested which apparently did not approve
themselves to the architects who made the restorations, for they only followed the writer of the old
history in part.   In the tympana of the two smaller
arches over the entrance are Herod directing the
massacre of the Innocents, and the Flight into Egypt.
Between them, above, is a figure of Christ giving the
blessing of the Trinity with upraised right hand, the
first and second fingers being upright and the thumb
crossing them in the conventional way for such a
blessing.

The spirit of all the ornamentation of this arch is

undoubtedly religious, and I do not wish to criticise it in any irreverent spirit, but the effect is so irresistibly comical that no true description of it can be given that leaves out the funny side. The expression of the wise man who mocks Herod would make the most melancholy of men laugh. It is a combination of a leer, a sneer, and general hopeless idiocy. Moreover, he stands on one leg, and twists the other leg about the one on which he stands. This twisted leg, if unwound, would reach I don't know how far beyond the limits of the bas-relief. It seems to have been modelled on some serpent of mighty proportions, suggestive, perhaps, of the one who tempted Eve in the garden ; for this would be quite in accord with the general spirit of the composition. The Flight into Egypt is nearly as funny, principally on account of the extraordinary construction of the donkey, whose legs are as much too short as the wise man's were too long. It is hard to understand the sculptor's lack of fidelity here at least, if donkeys were as numerous in this part of the world in his day as they are now, but the artist's power was not sufficient to reproduce accurately even what he saw about him every day. His aim may have been to conventionalize for the sake of properly ornamenting spaces that needed ornament, but faithful reproduction was in any case out of his reach.

The funniest part of the whole conception is the figures which adorn the two principal arches. On the outer one, which is, of course, the larger, are thirty-four figures, and they are apparently all variations on one theme. The only name I could think of, that was in the least appropriate, was " A Study in Stomach Aches." I did not know that the agonies of violent colic could be portrayed in so many different ways. Sometimes both hands are on the stomach; sometimes one is uplifted as though in protest against the pain; sometimes both uphold the bowed head. The legs are drawn up and contorted in all kinds of ways. I am quite at a loss to account for this extraordinary choice of subject. Perhaps there was a plague once at Morlaas and the stricken ones came to be relieved at the church. Perhaps they had taken too much of the wine of the country, whose extreme acidity would amply account for the most violent pains.

At all events, the sufferers ought to be healed if the august people who adorn the arch just beneath them can do anything; for these are kings with crown and sceptre, and they are praying with all their might. It must be that these royal people are interceding vigorously for the tortured ones above them. Unless there is some such connection as this between the two arches, there is no coherence of subject at all, nor any possible explanation.

These figures, comical as they are, are neverthe-less very decorative, and they suggest that style which afterward came to such magnificence in the glorious façade of Amiens cathedral.

I think there may have been niches below for larger figures. At all events, blocks of stone unsupported by columns protrude so curiously from near the bases of the arches that they make it certain something must once have been below them, whether columns or figures in niches I cannot tell.

The façade is by far the most interesting part of the church. The interior does not compare with that of Lescar, for it is not Romanesque at all, except in the restored parts, but clearly Gothic of a very early half-formed style. Three of the old chapels have been restored in the Romanesque man-ner, and these are quite splendid in color, being decorated from floor to topmost arch with red and blue and gold. But, on the whole, the interior is not interesting. The Gothic has not been well united with its predecessor, and the result is somewhat con-fusing.

What a pity that Centulle's church could not have been preserved as it was when he built it! If it had been, we might have learned more about the early Romanesque of France here than from any other existing building that dates from that time.

But even as it is it harmonizes in some curious way with the forms of the mountains that surround it, and as I rode home again down the hill of Morlaas, and along the valley of the Gave de Pau, and looked at the great peaks beyond the river there was in my thought a most singular mixture of the rounded forms of the mountains and the round arches that bend over the portal of Morlaas' church.

I

CHAPTER XIV

THE CHÂTEAU OF HENRY OF NAVARRE

THE château in which Henry of Navarre was born is a very ancient building. It was begun in the tenth century. Unfortunately, but little remains of the original structure, although there is enough to indicate clearly the outlines of its construction.

The man who first made this place a fortress-castle was Gaston de Foix — usually called Gaston Phœbus, because he adopted a blazing sun as the emblem for his coat of arms. No one knows exactly why he chose the sun for his emblem. It was certainly an ambitious thing to do, because it naturally suggests that he thought he might outshine others. Some think the emblem was chosen because of the physical beauty of the man, which was certainly most remarkable ; but personal vanity would hardly carry him to such an extreme, however handsome he may have been. Others think it was because his success in war was so great that he was entitled to outshine any soldier of his day. It may be that he

THE CHÂTEAU OF HENRY OF NAVARRE

chose the sun for his emblem because it had so much
to do with the beauty of his castle.

The châteaux in the valley of the Loire, and by
the banks of the Cher and the Indre, are surrounded
by natural beauty of a very unusual kind, but there
is no one of them — not even Chinon — that com-
pares in loveliness of surrounding scenery with the
château on the hill crest above the Gave de Pau,
whose outlook is first across the river valley, then
upon the "coteaux" that rise slowly, gently, one
behind the other, and at last upon the full splendor
of the snow-clad Pyrenees. Upon these "coteaux"
are the vines of Jurançon, the oaks of the Pyrenees,
— a foreground for the picture of snow-clad peaks
behind them, seen against the blue sky of the south,
that cannot be seen anywhere else.

The château of Pau was already an old castle
when Henry IV. was born there. It was a very
stern castle then. There were five great towers.
These were connected by buildings in which were
the lodging and reception rooms, and the state
apartments. It was almost triangular in shape,
because it followed the natural formation of the hill
on whose top it stands. There were formerly ramparts around the castle, and a moat that was far
below these. In the old days, when this place was
really a fortress, it must have been far more pictu-

resque even than it is to-day, for then the houses
clustered about it, and the great church of St. Martin was not far from the drawbridge that gave
entrance close by the tower of Gaston Phœbus.
The tower is still here, built of the bricks that were
made on the banks of the Gave, and the stones that
were found in its valley. Now most of the castle
has been rebuilt in gray stone, but this harmonizes
beautifully with the green trees all about. The
moat has been filled up, but it has become one of
the most charming of gardens, where the people
walk and the children play.

Jeanne d'Albret, the mother of Henry of Navarre,
might have liked to see the people wandering in
these gardens, and even in her ancient halls, for
she loved the people more than any other princess
of her time. She was quite unlike the women at
the court of the French king. She had an intelligence superior to theirs, and a simplicity of mind
and courage, both physical and mental, of which they
knew little and cared less. Some say that she was
poisoned because her virtue was a rebuke to those
who were living licentious lives.

When Henry IV. came into the world his mother
sang the song of the Béarnaises, in which they ask
to be the mother of a man. When her child was
born, and his grandfather had taken him in his arms

and in his way christened him with Jurançon wine, his education became at once her task. She treated him not as if he were a king, but more as the children of Béarnais peasants are treated.

The king's boyhood was spent among the mountains at Coarraze, where he was brought up as a real child of the people. Later he came back to the castle at Pau. He was a hardy peasant then in his strength and in his simple way of living, but he was already beginning to be a soldier. Later, in the gardens and parks of his castle he learned to love with all the ardor of the south. Gabrielle d'Estrées could tell of this side of his character. He loved her deeply, and she might have been his queen if the same poison that may have killed his mother had not killed his lady-love also.

He must have retained something of his simple habits, however, even in the great castle. It is said that one of his peasant friends came there once to visit him. This farmer of Béarn does not seem to have been frightened by the splendors about him. On the contrary, he was afraid his prince was about to starve. There is a custom in this country almost universally observed, that is, to hang the provisions for the winter on the rafters of the kitchen, which was also the dining-room. This custom is still the same as in the

time of King Henry. Hams and sides of bacon,
perhaps a boar's head, whatever vegetables could
be thus kept, might be seen hanging from these
rafters in the house of any well-to-do farmer in
the time of Henry IV., and they can be seen
there now. The king's peasant visitor was astonished because he did not see them hanging from
the ceilings of the palace. He said, "Sieur, surely
one will die of hunger here, because you have no
provisions on the ceiling." I give the literal translation, because it best expresses the intimate relation between the king and his subjects of Pau,
who hardly knew he was a king in those earlier
days, but thought of him as one of themselves,
now a man of full stature but who was just the
same person whose boyhood had been spent at
Coarraze among the mountains, and who seemed
there a peasant and a mountaineer as they were.

Although there were no provisions hanging from
the raftered ceilings of the castle of Pau, they
were, and are, nevertheless, very beautiful, much
more beautiful than those of the peasant's farm-
house, though built upon nearly the same model.
Many an English and American home has found
the suggestion for its dining-room ceiling from the
halls of Pau, not only the dining-room and the
kitchen, but the other great rooms which are **very**

fine and must have been even more picturesque before the restoration of them in the time of Louis Philippe.

The beds in this castle are as interesting as the raftered ceilings. That one which is said to have been the bed of Jeanne d'Albret herself, is superbly carved in ancient oak. Upon the side near the pillow is a recumbent figure that seems to be asleep, but, nevertheless, it is called the "guardian angel of the bed." There is something so curious about a guardian angel being asleep that I looked again and again to make sure that such was the truth. Alas! it is indeed the fact, and yet Jeanne d'Albret seems to have been well taken care of by the higher powers.

The most artistic beauties of the interior are not in the ceilings or the beds, but in the tapestries, which are simply superb. They are mostly Gobelin work, but there are some from Beauvais. It would take too much time to describe them all, for they fill the great halls and the smaller chambers too. They are nearly everywhere in this castle. Many of them are justly celebrated for their beauty of color and some for their interest in grouping and picturesque suggestion of some scene. That one that represents Henry IV.'s parting with Gabrielle d'Estrées is one of the most striking. It is almost like a fine oil painting and in its action it is extremely dramatic.

Bernadotte, the king of Sweden, is closely associated with the château of Pau. He was born not far from it, and he has enriched it with many costly and beautiful things, most of them made of the marbles of Sweden, some of which are very fine in color. The king who became a Protestant that he might come to the throne of Sweden and the other who became a Roman Catholic that he might be king of France are brought close together in this castle.

The cradle of Henry of Navarre is in the château of Pau. It is a tortoise shell, and it was one of the great treasures of all the southern kingdom when Henry became king of France. There is a story about how it was saved at the time of the Revolution. A certain M. de Beauregard was afraid that this precious relic would be destroyed by the soldiers and the mob, and he resolved to save it if he could, even at the peril of life itself. He took it from the castle to his own home, and substituted another tortoise shell for it in the castle. This one was destroyed by the revolutionists. When the fever of their wrath had subsided and there was again a monarchy in France, he put the king's cradle back in its place. The story may be true.

At all events, the Duchesse d'Angoulême believed it, for she embroidered the banners that are now about it. This work of the daughter of Louis XVI. and Marie Antoinette was supplemented by a gift from Louis XVIII. of a gold helmet surmounted by white plumes, meant to be as nearly as possible like the helmet of Navarre and the plumes that were to be the oriflamme of France on the day of Ivry.

The chapter of history that was begun in the château where Henry IV. came into the world was a very strange one. The strong, proud mother exulting over the birth of her son, the grandfather, hardly less proud, christening him with the wine of his native land and declaring that he was to be a right noble king, and a true Béarnais, the babyhood days in the tortoise-shell cradle, the years of boyhood among the peasants at Coarraze, the early battles when this youth showed himself a better soldier than some of the oldest warriors of France, the grand battle of Ivry, the final conquest of Paris, — all these had their beginnings in this room at Pau.

The spirit of Jeanne d'Albret is one of the noblest in French history. During her absence the castle was attacked by the Biscayans, under Terride; when she returned the assailants were defeated. Strangest thought of all about this place, she pardoned those who had rebelled against her and would have killed her if they could.

In spite of the influence of such a life as that of Jeanne d'Albret, Henry did not live a moral life. It must have shocked his mother to see him walking about the castle with one of his mistresses. She must have been shocked, too, when Marguerite came here, and the life of the court became even worse than before. It seems strange that this strong noble woman should have been thus afflicted. It is her spirit even more than that of the hero of Ivry, the great king of France, that dwells in the castle at Pau. It is not quite the same as the inspiration of Chinon by Joan of Arc, but there is a most ennobling influence in it that comes from the thought of motherhood, the true woman who cared for her child and trained him so far as she could toward the development of his powers. With the thought of her it is possible to leave the château with all its magnificence within and without, and come into the glorious beauty of the valley and the mountains, feeling that she belonged among them and that her presence in the castle has brought it into close sympathy with the snow-clad peaks that rise about its terraces.

CHAPTER XV

AT Chinon the interest is centralized about Joan
of Arc and Charles VII. At Langeais Charles VIII.
and Anne of Brittany are those most closely associated with its history. It was here that they were
married in the great hall which is now the salon
of the château. It is not only the historical associations that make Langeais interesting; there is,
beside, the beauty of the place itself and the charm
of the drive to it from Tours. Langeais is not a
long way from the city of St. Martin and Louis XI.
The road follows the Loire, and there are pictures
such as Daubigny might paint at every turn, but
this greatest painter of the river scenery of France
preferred the Seine. I wish he had painted the
Tour de Cinq-Mars that is on the way from Tours
to Langeais. This tower stands quite alone. It
must have been once a part of a larger building, —
a Roman structure, as some think. Its loneliness
now is most significant. It seems to tell how Cinq-

Mars stood alone on the scaffold when his king had forsaken him and Richelieu had doomed him to die. It is a strange episode in history. Cinq-Mars was not only the king's favorite, but his power at court was so great that it was only next to that of the king himself. If he had been faithful, he might have been one of the heroes of France. He had courage enough, but he lacked judgment, and his head was not sufficiently strong to withstand the influence of the flattery that the courtiers daily gave him.

His life, short though it was, gives a marked contrast to the lives of those who lived near his tower. Following the road a little farther, the hills by the river-side become higher. There are cliffs of white stone. In caves in these cliffs were the homes of the people, while Cinq-Mars was a favorite at court. Cliff-dwellers they were then, and some of them are so now. Taine says that the people lived in caves in the time of the luxury and splendor of Louis XIV.'s court. On the banks of the Loire between Tours and Langeais it is easy to see that this is the truth. Although there are these sad associations with the landscape, there is also much beauty. The winding road by the river-side gives an ever-varying view of field and hill-slope, of orchards and vineyards — a smiling land

THE CHÂTEAU OF LANGEAIS

of plenty and content it seems. It was a land that
Anne of Brittany loved. It was her home, and she
thought it almost a kingdom in itself. She was very
ambitious, and she even thought at one time of a
marriage with the king of Spain. This did not
come to pass, but she married two kings of France,
— Charles VIII. and Louis XII. Even then her
cup of joy was not full, for her children died and
no heir to the throne of France came from her.

Two great towers flank the entrance to Anne
of Brittany's château of Langeais. They are round,
with small openings here and there, and they have
the curious, conical top so characteristic of the
French architecture of that early time. The drawbridge is still there that leads to the gateway, and
even now it can be lifted up by the long iron chains
that are attached to beams projecting from the wall
just as it was in the olden time. When it was
lifted it became a defence instead of a way of
access, but there was still another defence a little
behind it, — the portcullis in the second arch of the
deep gateway. Even from the entrance it is easy
to know that Langeais was meant to be a fortress
as well as a home. The walls on the side where
this entrance is emphasize this thought, for they
are very high and in their lower part hardly pierced
at all by windows. The architecture of Langeais

is in the very first period of the transition from
the feudal stronghold to the luxurious château.
For this reason it is most interesting and quite as
well worth study as any château in Touraine, although there are others more beautiful. One of
the truths of mediæval history is admirably exem-
plified here in the same way as at Chinon and at
Loches. The houses come as close as they can to
the castle. They would even cross the moat if it
were possible, for the nearer the people came to the
home of a feudal lord, the surer they were of protection in case some other lord attacked him and
tried to ravage his domains.

And yet when the drawbridge is passed and the
court entered, the beauty of Langeais is so impressive that even Chenonceaux and Azay-le-Rideau
hardly surpass it.

Within there is no suggestion of the warlike aspect
of the exterior. It seems to be a home, a lovely,
most charming place to dwell in. In the inner
court there are three towers. The tops of two of
them do not rise far above the roof line, but the
other one is a lofty tower, almost as if bells should
be there as in cathedral towers to give a call to
worship. The beauty of the windows is almost
as remarkable as that of the towers. They are
richly ornamented, and they blend most pleasingly

with the slope of the roof and its sky line, which
here and there they break, not abruptly, but with
the hope that it might not be monotonous because
of uninterrupted length. Within the court of Langeais is a garden a little formal in arrangement, but
the terrace by its side commands a glorious view.

In the older times there was a great castle near
where the château of Langeais now stands. It was
situated upon the very top of the hill, considerably
higher than the present castle. What is left of it —
a few ruins of walls, a few statues more or less
broken — is within the grounds of Langeais. The
view from the hill crest where the old castle stood
is as magnificent as that at Chinon. It is the same
kind of scenery, — the majestic river, the purpled
vineyards, the grace of the many-arched bridges
spanning the river here and there from one horizon
to the other, and catching with their many arches
almost the very form and spirit of the river itself.

The present owner of Langeais has restored it,
and made it as nearly like the old building as he
could. In this he has been successful, and it was
not an easy thing to do, nor would many men wish
to live in rooms of the thirteenth-century manner
of domestic architecture. It is curious to think of
children of our own day sleeping in beds that are
as nearly as possible the same as Anne of Brittany

used herself and put her children to sleep in. The
unhappy queen lost her children, but for a little
while at Langeais the babies were in beds such as
are there now.

The hall in which Charles VIII. and Anne of
Brittany were married is unaltered save by the addition of exquisite carved furniture and rugs, superb
in color, and soft and rich in texture. This is now
the parlor of the mansion, and there are few more
interesting salons in Europe, partly because of the
beauty of it and partly because of its associations.

On the battlements above this beautiful room is
even now a picture of war in the mediæval time, for
all along their course about the castle are the loopholes for the archers and the narrow openings for the
pouring down of the boiling oil that was so potent a
weapon in the warfare of those days.

After seeing all this, we went out from the gate
of the tower-flanked portal by the drawbridge; and it
seemed like stepping almost in a moment from the
days of old to our own time.

We followed the winding river back toward
Tours; and as the towers of the town began to rise
in the distance above the line of Tours' great bridge,
the sun set in a glory of vivid gold, and made the
river as golden as the sky. Each arch of the bridge
had its reflection in the softly lighted water. Softer

and softer became the tones as darkness began to fall. Farther and farther away seemed the days of Anne and of Charles, which had come again to life for us for the little time we were at Langeais.

It was only one day, but we dreamed and we wondered, as we passed over the majestic bridge, in what age of the world we were living.

K

CHAPTER XVI

CHENONCEAUX AND AZAY-LE-RIDEAU

THE châteaux of Chenonceaux and Azay-le-Rideau are closely associated in the style of their architecture. It is a peculiar style, not known by any distinctive name unless it be called French Renaiscence, which would imply an earlier origin for that style than is generally given to it. The best definition of it would be a French fortress made into a palatial home. There is still something of the mediæval thought of defence, but there is not much of this. For the most part, beauty has taken the place once held by the stern defences of the French castles. The reason is not far to seek. When these two buildings were made, the feudal lords did not have need to defend themselves against a foreign foe or even against each other. The English had been driven away from these fair lands of France and Louis XI. had made a kingdom where before were warring barons, and no unity of national life.

It is curious how quickly the thought of beauty

THE CHÂTEAU OF CHENONCEAUX

came after the feudal fort was no longer needed. Some think that Chenonceaux and Azay-le-Rideau are the most beautiful buildings of their kind in the world.

The change from the defensive to the ornamental architecture is interesting. The forms and lines of the old castles were retained to some extent, but they were adapted to a different purpose. The sterner features are left out and only what is beautiful or strong in the older way of building is retained. The archers' loopholes give place to beautiful broad windows with carved ornaments in stone about them. The drawbridge is replaced by a structure of stone with sculptured lions about it.

Azay-le-Rideau is very peculiar in shape. The main part is almost square, but there is a wing which comes from it at a right angle and this is first seen after crossing the bridge of the lions. At every corner are round towers with conical tops. They are of white stone and the roofs are of blue slate. All about are great trees that in the days of autumn are yellow and orange and green that is less brilliant than in summer. There are many vines about the bridge and the balustrades of the terraces, that are brilliantly red like the woodbine and the sumach in October.

All these colors are not seen once only. Both

nature and art so delight in the charm of them that they must needs be repeated in the waters of the Indre that flow all about Azay-le-Rideau.

Looking upon this château and what is about it on one of those days of autumn sunshine, the first and almost overpowering effect is that of color so exquisitely harmonized, so often repeated in note after note of the same chord, that for a while one cannot think of any other beauty. But afterward a beauty of form is found that is in harmony with the color charm. The building is exquisitely proportioned. It has the same dignity of restfulness that is in a perfectly modelled statue. There is another charm of form that comes from the gabled windows different in height, and the rich sculptures about them.

Thus the whole picture is gradually unfolded, and when it has been enjoyed as a whole comes the pleasure of seeking out the beautiful things in the detailed work all about the building. The ornament everywhere is as rich as it can be without interfering with the general effect. In making his ornament subservient to his lines, the architect of Azay-le-Rideau agreed with the Gothic builders, but there is no other suggestion of Gothic here.

When the picture of this place as a whole and in its detail has been enjoyed, admired, studied perhaps,

there comes a thought about the river. Why does it
wind about the walls of this stately home? It must
be because the feudal way of building here had not
only its suggestion of tower or machicolation modified and made into ornamental forms, but also had to
do with the choice of site; for the river would have
served for a moat in mediæval days, and when it did
not flow of itself it would still be able to fill a moat
if one was needed.

The rivers and the hills determined the site of
many a castle in Touraine. In these that were built
later than the ancient strongholds, the beauty of the
water was counted upon as much as its defensive
use. The architect knew that the natural mirror
of a placid stream would double the charm of his
building. It does more than that, for reflection in
water is not mere repetition. There is something
dreamy about the way it gives back its thought of
all that is about it.

The lines are reversed and there is almost always
a little movement that softens the outlines, melting
them into an indistinctness, an ever-changing uncer-
tainty, delicious to an artist or a poet.

For this reason, as well as because of the beauty
of the building itself, the view of Azay-le-Rideau
from the side of the Indre opposite the gate of entrance seems to me one of the most beautiful views

of a perfect building, perfectly situated, that can be seen in all the world.

And when one wanders through the park, following paths shaded by great forest trees, and here and there crossing the river on a picturesque bridge catching almost at every turn some glimpse through the leaves of the white château, the blue turret tops, the green lawn, the balustrade with its crimson vine, the whole scene takes a place quite its own. There is but one Azay-le-Rideau.

No wonder this was a home for pleasure, and when the kings and the nobles came here, as they often did, it was for rest and relaxation. Their sterner work was not done here.

Here, doubtless, the charm of woman was supreme, but there is no one woman so closely associated with Azay-le-Rideau as was the case in several of the other famous castles.

Francis I. and Louis XIV. often came here, and it is easy to imagine they must have brought charming company with them.

The historical associations of the château are more connected with Francis I. than any other of the French kings.

This pleasure-loving but most able king had more to do with the building of the French châteaux of this time than any one else. Not only did he build

new ones, but he remodelled some of the others.
There are many traces of him at Azay-le-Rideau,
both without and within. Above the main entrance
are beautifully carved his salamander and the ermine
of Claude of Brittany, his wife. Over the chimneypiece in the library, which is a very beautiful work
of sculptural art, the arms of Francis are carved.
There is a room called the "Chamber of the Kings,"
where the monarchs slept when they came to Azay-
le-Rideau.

In this room was once a fine portrait of Catherine
de' Medici by Clouet, but this has now been hung in
one of the rooms on the second floor. The collection
of pictures here is very large and extremely interesting, but unfortunately the ordinary visitor is allowed
but little time to see it, for the château now belongs
to the Marquis de Biencourt, and it is only by his
courtesy that visitors can enter at all.

Even in the short time one has to look at the pictures a great impression is produced by them. Francis I., Calvin, Mary Stuart, Henry II., Charles IX.,
Marguerite of Navarre, the venerable Coligny, the
Maid of Orleans, Anne of Austria still striving to be
beautiful, and showing off the "fairest hand and arm
in France " — all these are here, and there are many
more beside them.

The house is full of the portraits of noble and

distinguished people. If they stepped down from their frames, they would make a goodly company indeed, as they walked about the halls of the castle or wandered beneath the trees of the park by the river-side. Many of them were great people, but even royalty has seldom found a more charming home than this many-towered white mansion by the banks of the Indre.

At Chenonceaux historical association plays so prominent a part that it should be spoken of even before the castle itself is described. This was the home of Diane de Poitiers, one of the most remarkable women in all French history. It was not built by her, although she added largely to it. Thomas Bohier and Catherine Briçonnet were the originators of it. Bohier should have finished it, for he gave money and pains enough toward building it, but he became a bankrupt, and his family were bankrupts also — all involved in the one misfortune. Then the property was forfeited to the crown.

When Henry II. came to the throne he gave this château to Diane de Poitiers, who had long coveted it. She used to come here on hunting-parties from Plessis-les-Tours, riding with the young Dauphin in the gay train of Francis I. It is natural to think of this famous favorite as a devotee of pleasure, but although very beautiful, she was hard and cold and calculating; extremely avaricious, and losing no opportunity to enrich herself, no matter at whose cost.

She was not satisfied with the king's grant of Chenonceaux, but caused legal proceedings to be instituted against the poor Bohiers, with the idea of deriving title through them. Curiously enough, she was successful in this, but the methods of the courts must have been open to question as to their honesty.

It may truly be said that the stain of stealing and of cruelty, cruelty that even pursues its victim to the very death, is on the walls of Chenonceaux. But Diane finally was the mistress there, and it became the central place of the luxurious, but somewhat romantic, life of the French court in one of the most interesting periods in its history. As one looks upon the exquisite beauties of Chenonceaux, it is not pleasant to think how Diane became their owner, but it is pleasant to think that her ownership was a short one; for Catherine de' Medici took it away from her, as soon as she could after the king's death, and sent her away to Chaumont, and then Catherine herself lived for a time at Chenonceaux. Other queens lived there too. Mary Stuart came there with her young husband, Francis II., and some of the happiest months of her troubled life were spent here. Anne of Austria and her son Louis XIV. were here.

One would have to mention every famous warrior in French history at that time, if the list were to be complete of those who loved to linger in the beautiful halls and gardens of this exquisite château.

But not only kings and queens were here. Later in its history the château was a resort for literary men. Rousseau and Voltaire, Diderot, Buffon, many of the greatest men in the French world of letters, were here. There are few buildings whose associations are more interesting than those of Chenonceaux.

The château is reached through a long avenue. It is straight, as the custom is in France, and it is over-arched by great sycamore trees; they are called plane trees in France. These trees are planted close together, and therefore not room enough is left for the growth of the lower branches. The verdure is all above, and it is supported by the two rows of tree-trunk columns as though it were one long arched roof. This use of trees, although too formal for the modern landscape gardener, has its own beauty, per-haps rather a stately dignity, which is very impres-sive especially when an avenue thus treated is as broad and long as it is here.

This avenue that leads to Chenonceaux is guarded at the entrance to the grounds by two marble sphinxes. In such choice of ornament at the very gate there is something quite suggestive of the char-

acter of this famous royal favorite. It may be that
Diane herself did not choose the subject for these
statues, and yet it is possible and thoroughly in keeping with her character that she did. If she did not
do it, some artist did who had failed to read the riddle
of her nature. The riddle of the sphinx is not harder
to read. Diane de Poitiers was apparently the very
source whence came the luxury and licentiousness
of a dissolute court, and yet she herself was utterly
hard and passionless. It is said that she never used
the paints and powders used too freely by the other
ladies of the court, but preserved her beauty even to
old age by vigorous athletic exercise patiently per-
severed in, and also by never allowing herself to be
disturbed by emotion of any kind. She rose early
and rode on her horse around the beautiful park of
Chenonceaux, at the time of the sunrise. Returning
to her apartment, she went again to her couch and
"gracefully déshabillée" transacted her business for
the day. Later she came, fresh and beautiful as ever,
to the fêtes and enjoyments of the afternoon and
evening. Diane de Poitiers must have had great
beauty of form if Jean Goujon's statue of her as
"Diana, the Huntress" at the château of Anet is
true. Probably it is; for that great artist would not
lie even to flatter, as many of them did. Her beauty
cannot be known about now, because the pictures and

statues of her do not agree. There seems to have been something of the Amazon about her, and something of Vivien, too, at the moment when she charmed Merlin under the gnarled oak.

After entering the gateway and passing the sphinxes, even the mysterious Diane is forgotten in the beauty of her home.

First rises in full view the tower of Catherine Briçonnet, the only part of her building that remains. It is circular in form with the conical top of the older fortress-châteaux, but the line of the cone is broken by a smaller cone similar in general outline, but not rising so high.

This tower is quite detached, and stands alone at some distance from the portal of Chenonceaux. The effect of it is not only almost indescribably picturesque, but full of that meaning which only a poet can fitly express. It seems like a sentry left by ages past to watch the castle gate, and there is a sadness in its loneliness because the watch it kept was in vain. It could not prevent the entrance here of what was unseemly, what would have been utterly abhorrent to the thought of Catherine Briçonnet.

But what this solitary tower guards, and even frowns upon, is far lovelier than itself, though not so strong. It is the château of Chenonceaux — one of the few buildings in the world absolutely unique, because it has little or no resemblance to any other, even of those that were built in the same time and with an effort at the same effect.

The beauty of the building is so delicate, so charming, that it seems like a realized dream. What dream might that have been? Possibly a thought of old French forts; but that would only have lasted a minute. Possibly something of the luxury and splendor of the Alhambra. That thought would have lasted longer; but even that is not all that might be dreamed about here. A castle that is built on arches over a river is so rarely seen that it makes any student of architecture wonder what was the impelling motive in the building of it.

Chenonceaux is built across the Cher. A part of it is on one bank, a part on the other; the long gallery connecting the two is on the arches over the river. Though built in this most singular way, the effect is not unlike that of Azay-le-Rideau. There is the same brilliant white of the stone, the same deep blue of the turret-cones, and there are the sculptured windows and the fine roof line, most artistically broken here and there by the tower or the gable over a window.

It is rather interesting to think that the construction of a building which was in itself almost an expression of the luxury of kings should have been

determined by the presence of a mill on the Cher
bank. The river turned the mill-wheel, the grain
was ground, there was food for the rich and the
poor; but the foundations of the old mill supported
later, long after its stones had ceased to grind, the
palace that bridges the Cher. It was not well that
the work of the mill should be stopped. A little
later in French history the kings themselves would
have been glad enough if the mills would give the
people flour for their bread.

Diane de Poitiers used these mill foundations for
her great gallery. Catherine de' Medici added to
the building which Diane had begun.

The Cher is quite a broad river here, and therefore the galleries that cross it upon the stone arches
are long. From every window in them is a view
up and down of the river and the meadows, the
noble trees, the vineyards, and the sloping hillsides
that come down to the river's bank.

But Diane de Poitiers was not content even with
such loveliness as this. She had to have a garden,
and she meant it to be unrivalled. It was an Italian
garden, surrounded by the carved stone balustrades
so familiar both in French and Italian pictures. To
its beauty the best gardeners of France gave of their
skill, and in its day it was thought to be without a
peer. Now it seems stiff and formal in its arrange-

ment, because landscape-gardening has become a different and a far more beautiful art in these days.

The situation of this garden was chosen with perfect taste, because from its walks and terraces can be obtained the most exquisite views of the château and the park about it, and the river flowing in the midst and repeating in its clear mirror every line of arch and turret, every color of tree, and meadow flower, and vine.

From here the roof of Chenonceaux can best be studied. I doubt if there is a more beautiful roof in the world. It is high pitched. The cones of the turret-tops are not far above the cornice, and therefore they are relieved against the roof itself. The chimneys, which are richly carved, spring directly from the roof with most charming variety of position and grouping.

What a picture it must have been when Henry II. and Diane de Poitiers, and all the courtiers in their gorgeous costumes, walked in this garden by the river, with the beauty of the castle just beyond. A Watteau or a Monticelli would have loved to paint such a scene. Isabey's palette of flaming colors might have rendered it even better.

At one time Chenonceaux must have been nearly as beautiful within as it was without. The rooms were large and finely proportioned, and the long gallery over the river was a very uncommon and interesting feature, especially when ornamented as it once was by superb statues, — antiques most of them, — and by many fine pictures. Beside all this, the walls of the rooms were hung with the richest tapestry. There were heavy, soft curtains over the doors, and the more stately rooms were adorned with armor and weapons, coats of arms and all those splendidly decorative things that belong to the feudal days.

Now, alas! it is all very different. Most of the fine works of art have been taken away and sold to pay the debts the owners of the castle owed to the state. There has been some attempt at restoration of these rooms and halls that in other days were so beautiful, but, unfortunately, most of this work is in bad taste.

Only a small part of the interior is now shown to visitors. Mary Stuart's room was not opened to us at all, and I could only catch a hasty glimpse of the apartment of Catherine de' Medici — a sombre room with heavy panelling, whose atmosphere seemed quite in keeping with the character of its occupant. What room in the château the fair Diane herself habitually used as a sleeping-room I could not find out.

But the interior on the whole is not as interesting as that of Azay-le-Rideau — nor is it comparable in charm to that of Langeais, which is perhaps the most delightful of all the Touraine châteaux so far as its interior is concerned, although it has not such associations with the most brilliant days of French history as has Chenonceaux.

In the evening the train slowly returns to Tours, and as we wait for its long-deferred arrival, there is plenty of leisure time in which one may reflect upon the singular beauty of the château and its surroundings, and also upon the extraordinary character of the woman who was so long its inspiring spirit.

L

CHAPTER XVII

CHINON

THE churches and the châteaux of mediæval France are closely connected in their history. There is also a religious spirit in both of them. It seems strange even to speak of religion in the same breath with the stories about what has been done in these old castles, and yet the fact is that war, religion, and sensuality are most curiously interwoven in the story of them all.

To the lover of history the castle of Chinon is more interesting than any other in the region of old Touraine, not because its historical associations are more numerous, but because they are centralized about the most interesting figure in French history — one of the most interesting in all history — Joan of Arc, the maid of Domrémy. It was at Chinon that she had her first interview with Charles VII., and therefore it is the thought of her more than of all the other great people who came to Chinon that inspires this place, filling it with a spirit higher

THE CASTLE OF CHINON

and more lovely than that of any other castle in France.

But Chinon was an old castle when she came to it. It is very closely associated with the Plantagenet kings, for it was a stronghold of Henry II. of England, and here he died. Richard Cœur de Lion and the other sons of Henry were all here, and some of the most tragic scenes between the king and his unruly sons took place at Chinon. When Henry died here, almost with his last breath he cursed the sons whom he said had killed him. At this château English and French history are more closely linked together than at any other castle in France.

Chinon is situated on a high hill which overlooks the valley of the Vienne. The castle was once of vast extent, but is now a ruin. Only enough remains of its towers and walls to show where it stood, and to trace with some approach to certainty the general arrangement of its halls and rooms, its ramparts, magazines and dungeons, and also its chapel. Before gunpowder was invented the castle was thought to be impregnable; for the hill on which it stands is very steep and high on three sides, and on the fourth side a deep chasm was artificially made that completely isolates it. The walls were very lofty and strong, and the massive towers rose far above these, thus giving means of defence that in feudal days could not be overcome. The town clusters about the base of the hill far below the castle walls, but it climbs up as far as it can toward the strong protector above.

There are spires among these high-pitched roofs of blue slate which seem almost like spires themselves. Where these spires rise were, and still are, the churches; and they are the very churches that were there in the time of Joan of Arc. When the inspired peasant girl climbed the steep path that led to the castle, she must have looked down upon just such a town as is there to-day; and she could see the church where she prayed before she went to see the king, and perhaps the house of the widow who sheltered her when she came to Chinon and waited until she could see Charles VII.

It may be that when she reached the height where the castle stands, she looked farther than the town, beyond its roof and its spires, and rested for a moment, — even although she was going to see the king with the purpose of delivering him from his foes, — that she might look upon the glorious landscape below and all about the hill of the castle, reaching even to the far horizon. If she did, then, look upon this lovely land, her heart must have thrilled again with patriotic ardor, and she must have once more vowed to deliver this sunny, fertile

heritage of the kings of France from the stranger
and the oppressor. It is now, and it was then, a
land of vineyards and orchards, of growing grain, and
of noble forests. Then as now the sparkling stream of
the Vienne came rippling down the valley from so
far away that its bright water seemed to touch the
brighter sky ere it left it to come hither. Passing
beneath majestic bridges with many stone arches,
the Vienne seems to linger long, serenely content
beneath the hill of Chinon. Reluctantly passing
the great castle, as though it were loath to leave it,
it passes beneath more stone arches, and wanders
amid more fields, until at last — a thread of silver —
it is lost again in the bright sky from which it came.

In all its long wanderings it was everywhere a
blessing; for the vines grew beside it, and the trees
bent over to kiss it, and the meadows throbbed with
more living green beneath its touch. Beyond the
valley rose low hills that encircled it, and these
were partly vine clad, and sometimes their slopes
were yellow with the ripening grain. Some of them
were dark with the shade of great trees. Here and
there the sentry poplars guarded the ways that went
from one happy hamlet to another, each with its church
spire. So far away were the broad fields one after
the other, and the low hills that were about them, so
long was the course of the bright river from where

it left the sky far away to where it joined it again, that this land lying here with one charm after another to delight the eye and lead it even to the horizon, seems in itself a kingdom, a great domain where people might dwell peacefully, and for whose safety one might be content to die, if sacrifice of life were needed to preserve its homes and fields.

Upon this scene looked Joan of Arc when she stood before the bridge that leads across the moat to the lofty Tour de l'Horloge. This high tower with machicolated battlements, with pinnacle at one end and turret at the other, is still standing more perfectly preserved than anything else which now remains of the ancient castle. Here the soldiers used to work the portcullis, and there is still a narrow slit in the wall through which they looked to see who was there before they would give admittance, and through this slit still looks the concierge to see what visitors approach. Here stood the peasant girl of Domrémy while the soldiers looked at her ere they raised the portcullis and let the drawbridge down. It must have been a strange moment, one of deep import even in the life of one who was accustomed to what was wonderful, what she herself thought to be supernatural, because if the bridge was lowered and the portcullis raised, she would soon stand in the presence of the king of France, and all that she had seen in her visions would begin to take on its earthly form.

The great hall in which Joan of Arc met the king was in the Château dù Milieu, a part of the castle that immediately adjoins the Tour de l'Horloge. This was not the part built by the English Plantagenet kings, which was called the castle and chapel of St. George. This English part was built to defend the one weak point of Chinon, the only place where its natural hill defence was not complete. All that the English had built was behind the Maid of Orleans when she passed beneath the portcullis in the Tour de l'Horloge and entered the great courtyard of the castle. What was before her was the French building, and it was there that the French king was holding his courts. There in lazy, luxurious idleness his time was spent, nor did he like to leave, even for a time, the caresses of his favorite to listen to one who came to tell him of the woes of France and to nerve him to such action as might redress them.

Truly the French part of the castle was before her and the English part behind. Truly at that moment the English page of French history was turned and the French one opened.

There is very little left of the great hall at

Chinon where Joan of Arc had her interview with
Charles VII.　One gabled end there is, and to this
is still attached at the height of the first floor the
chimneypiece before which their interview must
have taken place.　Even this is partly in ruins,
but enough remains to show its general form and
appearance.　The kitchen, the armory, and the
common hall, or living room, were beneath the
grand hall of the king.　Nothing remains of any
of these except fragments of walls and foundations
by which the general outline and arrangement can
be traced.　All of these rooms were on the side of
the castle facing the Vienne and its valley, and
from every window could be had that glorious view
of river and field, valley and hill slopes, of which I
have already spoken.　One of the fairest provinces
of France was at the feet of the king and the maid
as they talked, and it must have seemed to reach
forth supplicating hands to them entreating them to
save it from the oppression of the stranger.

Joan of Arc stayed at Chinon more than a
month, and while there she was lodged in the
Tour du Coudray.　This tower is a part of the
old fort of Coudray, which was the farthest west
of the three fortresses that crowned the hill.　It
was one of the inner towers, and did not command
the same magnificent view as the towers on the

valley side of the fortress. Originally, it was a lofty tower with three stories of rooms in it. The upper part is in ruins, but the room of the maid remains much as it was, and the staircase leading to the upper room also occupied by her is partly preserved.

Not very far from this tower are the ruins of the chapel of St. Martin, where Joan of Arc prayed after her interviews with the king. It is said that her supplications here were long and fervent, and they seem to have been greatly needed; for it was very hard to arouse the sluggish, pleasure-loving king. He did not want to fight; he wanted to enjoy himself. Little he thought about France; much he thought about the favorites who surrounded him. It seems almost a miracle that he ever was aroused from this lazy, luxurious life, and that he did at last give the peasant maiden her armor, put her white banner in her hand, and follow her to battle. How those who lived in that licentious court must have felt when they looked upon this pure maiden, who was a living rebuke to them! How they must have slandered her to the weak king, a voluptuary himself and quite willing to lend his ear to any tale of scandal! It is no wonder that Joan of Arc had to pray for a month in St. Martin's chapel.

The wonder is that at last she was permitted to
go in her king's name, bearing his banner, to rescue
his country and hers, and to turn backward the tide
of English invasion which had well nigh overflowed
all the land of France.

Enough remains of the ruins of Chinon to tell
what Joan of Arc's life must have been during the
month she dwelt there. It requires but little imagination to rebuild the walls and towers, even the
chapel, and to people them again with the characters
so well known in history, among whom she moved
during her stay in the castle.

In all France there is no more fascinating place in
which to linger and to dream. I might not be wrong
if I called it a sacred place. It is now a shrine since
Joan of Arc may be called to be a saint by the
Roman Church. But this religious inspiration is not
all of the spirit of it. The glorious landscape has its
part also.

Passing from the great hall along the ramparts
and coming to the Tour de Boissy and the Tour du
Moulin, this wonderful view is seen in ever-changing
lights. Sometimes a part of it is framed in a ruined
window. Sometimes but a little can be seen through
some narrow opening used by the archers. Again from
a tower-top the whole vast prospect bursts upon the
astonished eye. The rush of thought and feeling at

once becomes bewildering. There is so deep an impression upon the mind and the senses at the same time that one knows not whether to shut his eyes and go back in thought to the intrepid maid, or open them and look upon one of the fairest landscapes of earth.

By the Tour d'Argenton, another of the great towers upon Chinon's walls, is a secret passage that led from the king's apartments to those of Agnes Sorel. This remarkable woman completed the work which Joan of Arc did not live to finish.

Agnes Sorel was one among the many famous women who have had so great an influence upon the development of France as a nation. It is true that she was the king's mistress, but it is also true that she inspired him to do the best and noblest things he ever did in his life. She sent him to battle. He left her to seek salvation for France and honor for himself. To the inspiration of her words, the magic of her presence, the wisdom of her counsels, must be attributed, in a large degree, the success of Charles VII. in finishing the work Joan of Arc began.

This woman was very beautiful. She was called " La Belle des Belles," — the very queen of beauty, —and her nature seems to have been as lovely as her person, for she was greatly revered by the poor and reverenced by the nuns and monks, whose churches and convents she munificently endowed.

The ruined halls and towers of Chinon are becoming more and more thickly peopled with those renowned in history ; but there are many more to come beside these who hold the chief place in the castle's story.

Louis XI. was here. Philippe de Commines was at Chinon. One of the last scenes in the time of the castle's glory was the entry of Cæsar Borgia. He brought the cardinal's hat for Georges d'Amboise, and he was well paid for doing it. In history, as in life, extremes meet sometimes. How can one think of Joan of Arc and Cæsar Borgia under the same roof ? They were there at different times, but Chinon sheltered both of them for many days.

After the Prince of Condé, one of the last of those who dwelt at Chinon, the château was given to Richelieu. He had so many castles that he could not live in all of them, and for some reason Chinon did not please him, and he let it fall into decay and ruin. There never has been any attempt at restoration in Chinon. There is not enough left of it to make possible such work as has been done at Carcassonne and Mont St. Michel. But for many years before its massive masonry crumbles to dust it will be eloquent of its story.

The two great towers of the castle are the Tour de Boissy and the Tour du Moulin. The windmill

tower is very curious, partly because of its singular
construction with double, apparently disconnected
tiers of arches inside, and partly because of its
position at the very end of the Château du Milieu,
where it would be more exposed to danger, in case
of an attack, than any other part of the castle. It
is strange to have a windmill on a fortress wall, but
it is stranger yet to have it in a place where it might
so easily be destroyed.

There are many old Roman statues, little figures,
fragments, in this Tour du Moulin, quite enough to
show that the Romans used the place as a stronghold.

The Tour de Boissy had once a conical roof like
the other towers of the old French castles, but this
has now disappeared and a flat roof of stone and lead
has taken its place. From the top of this tower can
be had one of the finest views of the old castle itself,
and also of the magnificent landscape of the valley of
the Vienne.

Following from this tower the line of the walls,
one comes to the entrance to the dungeons, of which
there were many, tier below tier, clear down to the
level of the valley. A dungeon is an article which
was in great demand in the days when the French
castles were built, and most of them had a large
and choice assortment of them. There were also
oubliettes at Chinon more terrible than the dungeons,

perhaps, although the lingering torture might be worse than the sudden plunge to death.

There is one more tower on Chinon's walls, — the Tour des Chiens, where the king kept his hounds. It has no architectural beauty, and there is very little of interest in it. Near this tower is the chapel of St. Mélaine, in which Henry II. died. As his end drew near, he was borne to this chapel that he might die before the altar.

So many pictures from the past had been before us during our day at Chinon that it was as delightful as it was unexpected to see one from the present.

As we stood in the Tour de l'Horloge, just above the gateway through which Joan of Arc entered, there came a sound of merry voices from below. Looking down from the tower window, we saw a bridal procession coming up the steep path toward the castle. It was led by the bride and the bridegroom, and the guests followed them. The concierge left us at once and went down to open the door for this gay party. When she came back we asked her why the brides came to Chinon, and she answered that it was a custom, a habit of many years, even centuries perhaps, for those just married to come with their friends and dance upon the smooth stone floor that is now the top of the Tour de Boissy. I asked her why they went there. She did not know. It

was a custom and had always been so ever since she
had been in the castle. It was not hard to discover
the reason for it. It was not because there is a glorious view from the tower, though happy brides might
find pleasure in looking upon such a scene on their
wedding-day. The reason why the brides come here
is that the spirit of Joan of Arc is in the castle. It
is here that her wonderful career began so far as the
king and his courtiers knew of it, although her visions
were at Domrémy in the little orchard by her home.
What maiden of France would not love to commune
with the spirit of Joan of Arc ere she set forth on
her own journey through life? Toward the highest
thought of what life may be, there could hardly be
a more powerful inspiration. The brides come here
that they may learn something of that spirit of devotion and self-sacrifice which made a heroine and a
saint of a simple peasant maiden.

CHAPTER XVIII

THE CHÂTEAU OF BLOIS

In visiting the castles of Touraine it is better to
stay a part of the time at Tours and a part at Blois,
because some châteaux are more easily accessible
from one place and some from the other. Blois has
a great advantage over Tours, because one of the
greatest of all the castles is here. After seeing
Chinon and Langeais, Chenonceaux and Azay-le-
Rideau, it seems scarcely possible that there could
be another Touraine castle capable of giving an impression quite different from that produced by any
of the others and in some ways more interesting than
any of them.

Blois is as overpowering in its beauty, as thrill-
ingly interesting in its historical suggestions, as if
there were no château but itself in all Touraine.
Like most of the others, it has its ancient history.
The Romans had a fortified camp here. Later the
early counts of Blois made the place a stronghold
wherein they might resist their enemies,—the counts

STAIRCASE OF THE CHÂTEAU OF BLOIS

of Anjou.   For ages what is now a château was a
fortress.

Its chief interest and its beauty do not come from
these earlier times.   Louis XII. was the first king
who tried to make Blois beautiful.   He built one
side of the court of which Francis I. built a second
and Gaston d'Orléans a third.

The fifteenth-century Gothic of Louis XII.'s part
of the building is a wonderfully beautiful example
of that exquisite style.

The entrance to the castle is through a portal
which is surmounted by an equestrian statue of this
monarch, man and horse fully armed ready for the
many battles in Italy wherein the king took part.
This statue is of gray granite, and the crown and
armor of the king and the trappings of his war-steed
are gilded.   It is an ornament most fit for the portal
of such a castle, whose greatness came from kings
and queens.

Not princes, or dukes, or knights, made Blois what
it is, nor had any but the kings much to do with it.
The part built by Gaston d'Orléans is a failure in
its exterior, and within it is even worse.   Not even
so great a duke as Guise could here resist the king,
though murder most foul alone ended his attempted
resistance.

Even while looking at this long building that

M

Louis XII. built of brick and granite with its perfect Gothic windows, one above the other, reaching far up toward the top of the high-pitched roof, with its lofty gateway in the same beautiful style and the martial statue above it with its wealth of carving, — its beauty of form and line, — it is hardly possible to think very much about it, because the place is haunted by the spirit of the murdered duke, and the first thought is not of its beauties but of the place where he was killed.

Nevertheless, the colonnade of Louis XII.'s building has much to do with this tragedy. It extends from the wing built by Francis I. to the chapel of Anne of Brittany.

When Henry III. and the Duke de Guise met in that time in December, 1588, a little before Christmas, their meeting took place at the bottom of the great staircase of Blois. They were going to the mass together in sign of friendship. To reach the chapel they had to pass in front of Louis XII.'s colonnade. The well-known picture by Comte, now in the Luxembourg, has for its subject this meeting.

The beauty of this colonnade may not have been noticed by either of them at that time, but it was there then as it is now. The king and the duke passed before its richly ornamented arches as they went toward the chapel. In the combination of the domestic and the religious uses of Gothic architecture, there are few things in the world more interesting than this colonnade and the chapel to which it leads. Its suggestion of the home and the church so closely brought together ought to have made Henry III. pause to think before he caused the Duke de Guise to be murdered under his own roof, and but a little while after that mass in the chapel, which was to be a solemn seal of friendship. The king did not pause, however, for even while he was in the chapel the "forty-five," D'Epernon's famous guards, were making their preparations for the assassination.

In the part of the castle built by Francis I. were the apartments of Catherine de' Medici and those of Henry III. The queen's were below those of the king. They have been restored and are now almost as they were, except for the absence of furniture. Enough remained of the ancient decoration to permit of its perfect restoration by such a master as M. Duban. The bedroom of the wicked queen is a long apartment with several windows that look out over the park and gardens of the castle, which were very extensive in the early days of the history of Blois, and are still beautiful. The floor of this room is of tile, and the beams of the ceiling are profusely ornamented with many designs in splendid color, amid which appears very often the letter *H*, the initial of Henry II., Catherine's husband. The crown, too, is often used with good effect in this decoration. Near by is the queen's oratory, the walls of which are panelled and ornamented with the most exquisite raised traceries in gold. Her private working-room beyond is similarly ornamented, and in these two small rooms there are at least three hundred ornamental designs, all executed in the same rich but most artistic way. It was in the bedroom of this suite of apartments that Catherine de' Medici lay on her death-bed, both before and after the murder of the Duke de Guise.

It was here that she implored her son not to kill him, one of the few times in her career when her voice was lifted upon the side of mercy and the sparing of human life. But Henry would not listen to her. He told his dying mother that she had taught him to kill his enemies, and kill them he would. What a strange thing for a son to say to his mother on her death-bed! What a parting thought of this world that must have been! And the queen writhed in her agony, and hoped that she might not hear the fall of Guise's body, because that would tell her the last deed of blood of her bloody life had been done.

Directly above the rooms where the dying queen lay are the apartments that were then occupied by her son, Henry III. The arrangement of the two suites of apartments is similar, and both are gorgeously decorated. There is a private stairway that connects the two and then leads up from the king's apartments to the roof. It was in this stairway that D'Epernon concealed his forty-five guardsmen. There were two private rooms in Henry's suite of apartments in which he received those with whom he wished to confer secretly, and where he worked himself when he wished to be quite alone. One was the old cabinet and the other the new. The Duke de Guise was asked to go to the new one. In turning from the door of the staircase to pass through the bedroom of King Henry, he was attacked from behind by the guardsmen who were concealed in the stairway. He made a gallant struggle for life, fighting all those who assailed him with wonderful strength and a spirit that knew no fear. At last he fell by the very bed-side of the king, and the queen, almost in her death agony below, heard his body fall and knew that the last of her lessons of bloodshed was carried to the end to which the others had been carried.

It was not long before this tragedy that Mary Stuart and her husband Francis II. had occupied these same rooms where this murder was committed. They were happy here, it is said, but they could not have rested peacefully if they had known what was to happen so soon in that very room where they lived and loved for a brief time.

It is not far from these gorgeous rooms to a prison cell in which was confined the Cardinal of Lorraine, the brother of the murdered Duke de Guise. The day after the duke was killed, the cardinal was summoned from his cell to meet the king. As he walked along the stone gallery with its richly carved balustrade that led toward the apartments of Henry III. he, too, was struck from behind and murdered. The bodies of these two Guise princes were burned, and the ashes strewn upon the waters of the Loire.

The Guises had been induced to come from Paris, where their chief following was, in order to attend a meeting of the States-General, which the king had called in the great hall which is at the angle of the castle between the parts built by Francis I. and Louis XII. This Salle d'Etats dates from the beginning of the thirteenth century, and has been restored by the same master hand that has brought the rest of the castle to life again. It is now one of the finest Gothic halls in Europe with its pointed windows, and its row of columns that divide it in the middle, and support the vault of a Gothic roof over each part.

It is splendid in red and blue and gold as it used to be. If the tapestries were there, the room would be nearly as it was when the Guises entered it, and the king came down the staircase that leads to it from the royal apartments.

It is better now, if one wishes to get a true idea of what the château of Blois is, to leave those parts of it which are so closely connected with the death of the duke and the cardinal, and look at it from quite another point of view. Although the great staircase that Francis I. built is associated with this tragedy because of the meeting of the king and the duke at the foot of it, there is no reason for suggesting anything about it, except its beauty. There is no such other stairway in the world, I suppose. The design of it is attributed to Leonardo da Vinci, simply for the reason that it is thought no other artist who ever lived would have been equal to such an achievement of the beauty and strength of architecture, combined with the most magnificent ornamentation. I believe there is no testimony of history that can be trusted telling that the wonderful genius of Leonardo really did this work, nor is there any that speaks of any other who did it. It has to tell its own story. It is also said that Jean Goujon did

some of the work of sculpture, but this also is a
tradition.   Certainly the exquisite statue of a woman
near the foot of the stairway suggests his handiwork,
but it must be trusted to tell its own tale.   The staircase is almost like a detached building about midway of the front of Francis I.'s wing.   It has not
the effect of a tower.   It is related in style to the
rest of this part of the château, and yet it hardly
seems to belong with it.   In the splendid ornamentation of its spiral staircase it would seem to belong
to the time of the Renascence, but it has Gothic
gargoyles, and its form throughout is not like that
of most buildings of the Renascence time.   It
seems to be almost *sui generis*, the exquisite
work of some genius who had his own style and
cared nothing for the schools.   Even in this wonderful work of art there is a suggestion of the wicked
queen who died at Blois, for Jean Goujon was killed
in the massacre of St. Bartholomew.

Although the staircase is so wonderfully beautiful,
it is not all of the beauty of Francis I.'s building.
The façade toward the courtyard is most richly ornamented.   The salamander, which was the king's
emblem, is repeatedly used, too often it may be, but
some of the representations of this curious creature
are masterpieces of the carver's art when it was great
enough to come close to that of the sculptor.   In

beauty of form and line this building does not equal
the Gothic part that Louis XII. built, but it is far
superior to the wing that Gaston d'Orléans entrusted
to Mansard. The style of this within and without
is in pitiable contrast with either of the others.
Nevertheless, Gaston must have thought it better
than the exquisite works of art that were before his
eyes here. He actually thought of pulling down the
whole castle and substituting Mansard's work. He
did destroy a good deal of it, but fortunately the
best part still remains.

Beside the three wings, the hall of the States-General, and the chapel of Anne of Brittany, there is still
another part of the castle of Blois. It is a very
ancient tower close to the ramparts that tell of the
fortress part the place once had in history. This
tower now stands quite alone. It was once a part of
the defences of Blois. Now the ivy clings to it and
seeks to conceal all harm that has been done to it by
time or violence. It has come to the days of a
peaceful old age. No longer does any foe attack it,
no longer does any restless, eager soul seek counsel
from the heavens on its top. It was hither that Catherine de' Medici resorted, and with her astronomer
consulted the stars. It was she who caused it to be
called "Uranæ Sacrum." Its position was well
suited for study of astronomy. High on the battle-

ments of Blois, which were themselves high above the town, there was nothing to hinder a view of the heavens from the horizon to the zenith. What terrible things must have been told of or suggested upon that tower top! Catherine and Louis XI. are alike in their superstition, their cruelty, and their professed zeal for the church. The astrologer who used the astrolabe here had a great influence upon the destinies of France — how much no one will ever know. Before any murder was committed or fearful crime of whatever nature, Louis XI. would pray and promise something to the Virgin or some saint, and Catherine would go to her oratory in a most devout manner, but before the fatal thing was done both would go to the astrologer and ask what the outcome of the intended crime was to be.

Upon this old tower of Blois what fearful things were thought of, what dreadful deeds decided upon! It may be the stars told Catherine that the Duke de Guise ought not to be murdered beneath her roof, but perhaps they also said her child was born a murderer.

It is very peaceful now. Far below is the church of St. Nicholas — a noble building of early Gothic work. The queen may have gone there to mass when she left the astrologer in the tower. Now as the sun sets the rooks come home to their nests about the towers of the church. There are many noisy greetings, much restless flying about, but at last the old church shelters them and they find peace. It was not so with Catherine — not on her tower, not in her oratory nor in the royal rooms of Blois, haunted by thoughts of blood and crime.

Below the church of St. Nicholas moves slowly, grandly on the Loire. Its peace is not disturbed by the evil that has been done upon its banks. It knows the secrets of the dungeons, the scaffolds, the assassin's knife; it could tell many a tale of unbridled ambition, of licentiousness that scarcely sought concealment, but it says no word. It tries to carry away its miserable burden of human woe and frailty, and bury it in the sea toward which it is eagerly going.

The sun has set. The rooks are quiet in their nests in the old church. The moon rises and silvers the river, the towers of the church, the town, the old observatory, the stairway of Francis, the colonnade of Louis. It shines, too, upon all the other châteaus by the Loire. To each it gives a touch of mystery, to all it gives a much-needed peace. Under its mystical light all the evil is forgotten, and only the exquisite beauty of the castles of Touraine remains in the mind.

CHAPTER XIX

THE CHÂTEAUX OF LOCHES AND CHAUMONT

LOCHES and Chaumont are so utterly different in construction, history, and spirit that I put them together in description for the sake of the contrast. Loches is on the river Indre. It takes about an hour and a half to reach it from Tours. Chaumont is on the Loire, and can be reached by carriage from Blois in about the same time.

To English people Loches may seem more interesting than any other of the castles of Touraine. Unless Chinon be excepted, there is no other château so closely associated with the early history of the Plantagenet kings. It was the ancient home of the counts of Anjou, and their chief stronghold in the wars that they waged year after year against the counts of Blois.

While Richard Cœur de Lion was away in Palestine, and his treacherous brother thought he would never return, John gave Loches to the French, but as soon as Richard was free after his imprisonment

172

he laid siege to the castle and took it. It was, however, retaken after a year's siege by Philip Augustus.

Loches is interesting also because Charles VII. long lived here, and there is a tower in which dwelt Agnes Sorel, the one woman whom he really loved. It was here, doubtless, that her courage, wisdom, and patriotic enthusiasm inspired Charles to go forth and complete the work which Joan of Arc had begun. The famous monument to Agnes Sorel is in the basement of this tower. It was formerly in the collegiate church near by, but the monks were afraid her life had not been pure enough to admit of her remains resting in so sacred a place. They did not seem to remember that she had endowed their monastery most munificently, and done many a good work for them, and therefore they asked Louis XI. to have her tomb removed from the church. That monarch, with characteristic acuteness, replied that they might move her body and her monument if they would give up the possessions they had received from her. It goes without saying that the tomb was not disturbed at that time, but later it was taken from the church and placed in Agnes' tower.

The monument itself, while not a masterpiece of sculpture, is very simple, and most touching in its suggestion. It is a recumbent figure with folded hands in the manner so common in the mediæval days, but it is varied from the usual type by the introduction of two little lambs at the feet and two angels, quite small, but beautifully chiselled, who bend over the face and seem to shelter it with their brooding wings. Agnes Sorel must have been a very beautiful woman if this is a good likeness of her, for even although it has been in places restored with plaster the face is most pure and lovely. It seems a strange monument for one who was a king's mistress, but it confirms the testimony of history that Agnes Sorel was a very high-souled woman and the king's good genius in the most critical days of his life.

It is not, however, the gentle Agnes who gives to Loches its chief historical interest. Not because she lived and loved here do people visit it to-day, but for the reason that Louis XI. had here his dungeons and torture chambers. These still remain, and they tell a tale of human cruelty which is hardly credible even when the eye looks upon those hideous cells whose mute testimony cannot be contradicted. The walls would be eloquent in themselves even if they were not covered with the written laments of many a prisoner who languished here for years until death finally came to his relief. These dungeons are in the older part of the castle, quite remote from Agnes' tower and Charles VII.'s royal apartments. Above

THE CHÂTEAU OF CHAUMONT

them looms up the gigantic donjon of Foulkes Nerra, half-ruined but still terrible and imposing. Around them wind the ramparts from which rises the Tour Ronde—still grim and defiant as in the feudal days. In this tower was the principal torture chamber. It is now used as the prison of the town. But there is another place in this tower far more terrible, and that is the dungeon down deep below the ground where Louis XI. kept Cardinal Balue suspended in an iron cage for years, just because he told some of the king's secrets to Charles of Burgundy. The dungeon is small. It is cut out of the wall of the castle, but the cage that hung within it was much smaller yet. A man could neither sit up nor lie down in it. A sort of crouching posture was all it would permit. There is a landing on the stairs just above this horrible place, to which Louis XI. used to come in order that he might see and gloat over the agonies of his victim.

Philip de Commines was also imprisoned at Loches for a few months, but his cell is not so horrible as that of Cardinal Balue. It is in another tower, and there was light enough for him to begin writing that history which probably gives as fair an idea as any of the character of Louis XI.

Within the great space enclosed by the ramparts of Loches, between the dungeons and the palace,

stands a church—the collegiate church, it is called—
which is thought to be one of the most remarkable
among the churches of France built at that time.

The peculiarity of it is that it has no roof in the
ordinary sense of that word as applied to churches,
for the nave is covered by four contiguous towers,
which are like domes, or, perhaps better, lanterns
when seen from within. I think the church more
remarkable than beautiful. It is a most interesting
study for an architect, but to the ordinary traveller
it is not especially attractive.

In spite of the great historic interest of Loches, it
is not a very pleasant place to visit. All that there
is of beauty of architecture, all the picturesqueness
of the houses with their high-pitched roofs climbing
up the hill to get as near the protecting castle as
possible, cannot efface the principal impression of
the place which comes from the horrors of its dungeons. It is a scene of crime and cruelty, of untold
agony, of tragedies almost beyond belief.

One breathes freer on passing out of its stern gate
and looking up at the blue sky the poor prisoners
could not see. As he sees again the sunshine, and
the fair fields and vineyards, he hopes the days of
the hideous tortures of the dungeons he has just left
are past, never to return.

How different the thought of charming Chaumont,

one of the fairest feudal castles in the world! Any
detailed description of such a place would not be of
much use—only a suggestion is needed to awaken
interest in it.

This was the home of Georges d'Amboise, the cardinal, Louis XII.'s great minister—the predecessor
of Richelieu and Mazarin. Here is his cardinal's hat
carved in stone over the door with Louis XII.'s
porcupine underneath it, and again, in the chapel
there is the throne he sat on, and the very famous
hat itself that Cæsar Borgia brought all the way
from Italy is hanging there over the throne just
below a great stained glass window, and the cardinal's cushions to sit on and to kneel on are all
there. Yes, everything is ready for him, and when
he comes in he will sit there on the throne, and
the hat will be placed on his head. Afterward
Catherine de' Medici and her ladies will enter the
gallery of the chapel by the private door, and there
they will sit on the cushioned seats with the high
carved backs, and hear mass, and doubtless partici-
pate in the ceremony with the utmost appearance, at
least, of piety.

In the rooms below are many things that make it
sure this must have been Catherine de' Medici's home
sometimes. Here is the queen's bed, with its richly
embroidered hangings and coverlid, just as it was

N

when she last rose from it to kneel at the prie-dieu by its side. There is the wash-stand, a rather elaborate one, on the other side. Upon it are all the implements of the toilet of a woman of that day — powder-box and rouge-pot, little bottles for essences and perfumes, a beautiful basin and pitcher, — everything in fact that was needed for this charming queen-mother's toilet. They are all in perfect order. Catherine de' Medici might use them now just as well as before, if her sphere of usefulness had not been changed from this world to another.

There cannot be any doubt that this was her room, when one sees it connects with an apartment used by the astrologer, Ruggieri. There is a portrait of the Italian astrologer in this room. There is his bed, — not quite so splendid nor so wide as the queen's, but good enough for any one. There was no prie-dieu beside it. He preferred, perhaps, to consult the stars.

There is a door opening from his room which gives entrance to the winding stone staircase that leads to the tower-top. Up this staircase the queen and the astrologer often went, that they might study the heavens together, and by their teaching decide the fate of many a poor mortal.

There is splendid carved furniture. There are coffers in which the treasures were kept, — exquisite works of Italian art. All these things tell that the

Italian queen lived here. The mistress of Catherine's husband, Henry II., Diane de Poitiers, lived here too after the king had died and Catherine had succeeded in stealing Chenonceaux from the royal favorite.

This château of Chaumont does not seem to-day as if it could have become the home of anybody, even if that person were the Duke de Broglie, who now lives there. Why, Voltaire was here! Georges Sand walked on these terraces, and wrote, perhaps, even in the Italian queen's room. The place was once a fortress. There was a moat. There are towers, with their loopholes for archers and arquebusiers, and the machicoulis, through which to pour down the boiling oil. There are ramparts.

The description of old Chaumont might be interesting, but what it is to-day is far more interesting, because it has become a home, — one of the most beautiful in France. Its white towers, with their blue-gray conical tops, rise from the crest of a hill far above the majestic Loire, broad and placid, moving on with great dignity and power among its meadows and vineyards and beneath the many arches of its bridges.

The towers are embowered in most luxuriant foliage. Trees climb up the hillside, and they even reach the castle. They surround it with living green. Sometimes when they have almost gained

the top they seem to try to vie in height with the
old white towers themselves. This they cannot do,
but the mingling of their varied greens with the white
and the blue-gray of the masonry is an artist's dream.

Nevertheless, it is not so romantic as the terraces
that overlook the river, for about these the vines
that love to climb have full sway. The ivy and
the honeysuckle, the clinging roses, even the mosses
and the ferns have claimed these ancient balustrades
for their own. They embrace and caress the old
stones. They almost hide them; but they do not
dare lift their flowers, nor even their leaves and
tendrils, high enough to shut out the Loire, a shining silver background for their beauties of color and
of form, as one looks down from the terrace.

A little lower down is the "lovers' walk," that
winds along the hillside, up and down, half hidden
by trees and shrubs, gay with flowers, and with
glimpses here and there of emerald turf, and sometimes of a pointed roof or tower far above, or a rip-
ple of sun-sparkled water far below, or of a bridge
that crosses the water so charmingly lighted.

This, then, is something of what Chaumont is to-
day, but it is only a suggestion. The historian must
tell what it used to be. Its charm as a home will be
remembered even if all the momentous facts in its
history are quite forgotten.

CHAPTER XX

THE CHÂTEAUX OF AMBOISE AND CHAMBORD

AMBOISE is one of the most interesting of the Touraine castles. Its exterior is most imposing, and its situation is charming; for it is on the crest of a hill beside the Loire, just at a point where a large island divides that majestic stream into two parts, thus adding an element of picturesqueness to the power and beauty of the river's movement. Its vast towers make it one of the most singular of all these châteaux. They rise almost from the level of the river to the top of the hill. The walls and buildings between the towers are dignified, and their turrets and pinnacled windows make a beautiful sky line as one looks up toward the castle from the banks of the Loire.

Although Amboise is so beautiful, it is, nevertheless, haunted, as Loches is, by some spirit that tells of the human agony there endured. It was here that the Huguenots were massacred after the conspiracy of La Renaudie and his followers against the Guises

181

had been discovered and frustrated. Catherine de' Medici, with her son, Francis II., and her other sons who afterwards became Charles IX., and Henry III., with her ladies in waiting and the young and beautiful Mary, Queen of Scots, all in full court dress, witnessed this horrible butchery from a balcony of the castle that faces the Loire. Above this balcony is another one, with an iron railing on which were placed the heads of the Huguenot chieftains.

It seems as if the incredibly wicked Italian queen simply waded in blood during the whole time of her baleful power in France. Once only, and then it was on her death-bed, she tried to stop the shedding of blood; but that scene belongs to the history of Blois.

An immense scaffold was built in an open square below the castle of Amboise, between the rock on which it stands and the bank of the Loire. The principal men among the Huguenots were led up hither together. They all sang in unison Clément Marot's translation of the psalm, " God be merciful to us and bless us." As the heads fell off one by one, the psalm grew fainter and fainter; but the last one kept on singing until his turn came to die. The headsman grew weary with his work. His axe was blunted, and at last he had to turn over the victims still left to other executioners. Many of

DOOR OF THE CHAPEL OF AMBOISE

the bodies were thrown into the Loire; but still there were so many of the killed about the streets, and even in the castle, that the court was obliged to leave Amboise on account of the stench that came from the unburied dead.

Such was one scene that Mary Stuart looked upon during her short married life with the young king, Francis II. She was to see many another scene of blood; but it is said that this one haunted her even to her dying day. She could not get rid of the thought of it even when she was preparing herself to die as the Huguenots died at Amboise.

Although this is the most striking and terrible page in its history, Amboise is really more closely connected with Charles VIII. than with any other king. He built a large part of it. To him is due the exquisite chapel, — one of the most beautiful examples of florid Gothic in the world, — which he built for his queen, Anne of Brittany, and dedicated to St. Hubert. The bas-relief over the door is of that familiar subject, — the saint meeting in the wood the stag with the miraculous cross between his horns. This is the work of Italian artists whom Charles VIII. brought back from Italy. The carvings within the little chapel are so exquisitely delicate that it seems as if the most dainty white lace, turned to cream-color by age, had been hung about the walls. So delightful is the little chapel on the edge of the terrace, with flowers and trees about it, that one almost forgets all about the big castle.

The castle, however, is a most interesting building, and in some ways quite unique. The towers and the chapel are not like those of any other château in Touraine. The great tower that is seen from the river-side is very famous, because it has within it an inclined plane which can be used for horses and even carriages. This leads from the level of the river to the apartments of the king on the hill-top. The noble people dismounted from their horses at the very doors of the rooms they were to occupy. There is another tower, similar to this one, at the farther end of the castle.

King Charles VIII. undertook these great works at Amboise partly to distract his mind from the grief which came upon him when his son died. This boy and his brother, the two children of Anne of Brittany, were buried in the cathedral of Tours, where their beautiful monument still remains. Charles's towers at Amboise became renowned all over Europe. Many a great king and warrior, many a lovely dame, ascended these inclined planes and dismounted in the courtyard of the castle. Among them were Charles V. of Spain, Francis I., Mary Queen of Scots, Catherine de' Medici, — most of the great people of France and many from the other kingdoms of Europe.

Charles VIII. at the time when he built Amboise was fonder of his building than anything else. He was so much engrossed in it that he wished to watch the workmen at their work as much as he could. In going to superintend their labors one day, he passed hastily under a very low, arched gateway that was between his private stairway and the ramparts. He struck his head against the stone arch and died a few hours afterwards from the effect of the blow.

If the interior of Amboise were as well preserved or as admirably restored as that of Blois it would certainly be one of the most interesting in all Touraine — but, unfortunately, this is not the case. The Comte de Paris, who owned the place, attempted to restore it, but succeeded only partly because of his banishment from France.

There is very little now to see within the castle, but the exterior is so fine, and the historical associations are so numerous, that Amboise will always be a favorite resort of the tourist who loves noble Gothic architecture, and cares to be in a place where some of the most interesting events in French history occurred.

Of Chambord I cannot speak with enthusiasm, although it is one of the largest of all the châteaux of this region. Francis I., for some reason or other, became tired of his work at Blois. It is astonishing that it could have been possible to become wearied with work at such a castle as Blois. It is said that if Francis had put the money he spent in building Chambord into finishing Blois, there never would have been a Versailles, because Blois would have been the permanent home of the French kings when they were not at Paris. Blois was left incomplete, and Chambord was built. The situation of this château is enough to make it less beautiful than the others even if it were in itself beautiful. Francis chose this place for his castle probably because of his fondness for hunting. On the site of Chambord was once a hunting-lodge to which the king often resorted. There is nothing of interest in the country immediately about this château now, but it must have been different when there was a great forest there. It may be that the king thought the place where he had found such pleasure in his sport would be always a charming place in which to dwell, but when the forest disappeared the charm was gone.

Chambord itself is not beautiful enough to dispense with the beauty of the forest trees that once were about it. The building is deplorably top-heavy. There are too many chimneys and they are too much ornamented. The upper and lower parts of the structure do not harmonize. When there was a moat about it the reflection in the water may have helped it, and given a different impression from that of to-day ; but even then it could not have been a harmonious building.

The most remarkable part of it is the staircase, which is very large and surmounted by a lantern of great size, though not of great beauty. This staircase is certainly most peculiar, even if it is not beautiful. There are two spiral stone stairways in it, arranged in such a way that people may ascend side by side and yet hardly see each other. The two stairways are separated by a slight difference of level, and one is inside the other. The stone supports, which are very massive, come between the two, and though the openings are many and large they are so arranged that through them very little is to be seen of one staircase from the other one. The effect is very curious, but it is far from being agreeable or artistic.

Nor is the château very interesting in its suggestions about history. Francis I. was here a good deal, but not in the most important days of his life. Louis XIV. was here too, but he seems to have been dreadfully bored at Chambord, and a good deal troubled about the quarrels of some of his mistresses. Madame de Montespan especially annoyed him here.

The most interesting person whose life is associated with Chambord is the Maréchal de Saxe, to whom the place was given by Louis XV. The hero of Fontenoy lived here for some time in great enjoyment of his luxurious surroundings; and he amused himself with reviews of troops and their manœuvres, which he directed from a balcony at the back of the palace. His excesses would soon have killed him if the Prince of Conti had not given him a mortal wound in a duel fought in the woods near the château.

At Chambord Molière's "Le Bourgeois Gentilhomme" was first produced before the court and the courtiers. Its success was immediate. There must have been a fine theatre here at that time in one of the halls that opens toward the great central staircase. Nothing is left of it now but the outer walls and the windows.

The vast château of Chambord is not without some interest, either of history or architecture, but it is far inferior in charm to any other of the important castles of Touraine.

On the way back to Blois, one may, if he pleases, visit two of the smaller châteaux, — Cheverny and Beauregard. The former belonged to a minister of Henry IV. It contains some very fine old armor, and there is a bedroom in it once occupied by King

Henry of Navarre. It is now nearly the same as it was in his time. There are also in this château some good pictures. The best of them are portraits. The subject of one is Cosmo de' Medici as a boy. Some think Van Dyck was the painter. Others ascribe it to Titian. It is a very fine portrait, worthy of either of the great men who may have painted it.

At Beauregard the chief interest is a very large gallery, the walls of which are entirely covered with so-called portraits of the kings and queens, the soldiers, statesmen, and the court beauties of Europe from 1400 to 1650. The pictures are so bad that it is hard to believe they can be likenesses, but nevertheless they are interesting because of their historical significance, even if only by way of suggestion.

From this château the drive back to Blois is charming. It leads through the vast forest where lords and ladies used to hunt with hawk and hound, and at last it comes again to the Loire, — the stream that seems to know all the secrets of the Touraine castles and yet remain calm and majestic.

CHAPTER XXI

ROMAN AND CHRISTIAN MONUMENTS AT NÎMES AND ARLES

NÎMES is now a busy French city, but it was once a Roman place. The early name of it was Nemausus. The Roman historians say little about it for some reason not yet fully understood, because it must have been a very important city in the western part of Rome's empire. Its amphitheatre is enough to show that it was large and populous, and its geographical situation easily explains its importance, for it was on the road from Rome to Spain.

The amphitheatre is in some ways even more interesting than the Colosseum at Rome. Its exterior is much better preserved. A large part of this is intact, even to the cornice where were the pierced stones in which were inserted the poles that were to hold up the awning that was spread over the seats of the spectators. It is not so high as the Colosseum. There are only two tiers of arches, but these are so lofty that they give the building an impression of

190

great height, and they are so massive that they speak in no uncertain tone of the strength of that Roman Empire of whose greatness they formed a part. One may walk all around the building under these vast arches, and it is possible once more to go all about it under the arches of the second tier. From here the view of the arena and the encircling seats is most fascinating. Rome seems to live again in this town of southern France.

The places of worship not only of the Romans but of the Greeks can well be studied at Nîmes. They offer a most interesting contrast to the Christian buildings, and it is well to study them with that thought in mind.

It is but a little way from the great arena of Nîmes to the Maison Carrée. What a pity they have given it a French name! It is not in the least French. It is Greek. Although it has come down from the days of Antoninus Pius, and Marcus Aurelius and Lucius Verus had something to do with the building of it, it is, nevertheless, distinctly Greek. Probably it was built by Greeks who came as colonists to many places in the Roman Empire after their own country had yielded to the irresistible power of the legions. Here at Nîmes they dreamed of the Acropolis as the Jews at Babylon did of Solomon's temple, but here they had the

opportunity, which must have been most delightful
to them, of reproducing one of their own Athenian
temples. The building is a gem of architecture. It
is small, as the Greek temples always were, but it is
nearly perfect in harmony of form and line. The
style is Corinthian. The columns of the peristyle
are very lofty, and their capitals most exquisitely
carved with that somewhat florid but deliciously
chastened ornamentation which marks the best
period of the Corinthian work. How the building
has been preserved in its present almost perfect
form is hard to tell. It was at first a temple of the
Greeks; then for a little time it was a Christian
church; afterward it became a stable, and the owner
of it at that time pared away the bases of the
columns a little in order to allow his carts to pass.
This seems to have been the worst injury the building has suffered. Afterward it became part of an
Augustinian convent, and was used as a burial-place.
Still later a tribunal of the Revolution held its
sittings here. Another change, and it became a
storehouse for corn, and last of all it was a museum,
and a museum it still is.

This temple is strongly contrasted in style with
the Nymphæum, once called the temple of Diana,
which is close beside the ancient baths. This is
a truly Roman building with the prevailing round

arch so characteristic of that style of architecture. It was here that those who had enjoyed their bath in the pure waters came to worship the nymphs of the stream and of the fountain that springs from the hill above it.

This most interesting building, though not so well preserved as the Maison Carrée, is, nevertheless, one of the most charming of the Roman monuments to be found outside of Rome itself. It has not been restored, and is partly in ruins, but remains almost exactly as it was more than sixteen centuries ago. The worship, the architecture, and the art of Rome can well be studied here. The noble cathedral of Carcassonne is not far from the Maison Carrée and the Nymphæum. The contrast tells its own tale as to the difference in the spirit of worship between the Roman and the Christian days.

It was not in the temples that the chief glory of Roman architecture was to be found. Not far from Nîmes is a monument that speaks as truly as any other of the power and the splendor of this wonderful people. The Pont du Gard is one of the most impressive of all Roman structures in the world. The arena at Nemausus needed water. Sometimes they flooded it, and had mimic naval battles as in all Roman amphitheatres of importance. This water had to be brought from a long distance and carried

o

over the hills and through the valleys by an aqueduct which was more than thirty miles long.

It is nearly fifteen miles from Nîmes to the Pont du Gard, but one scarcely tires of the long drive because the road itself is a Roman monument. Broad, smooth, majestic, it seems to flow on like some grand river that pays no heed to mountain, cliff, or any other obstacle, but quietly, albeit irresistibly, pursues its own course and eventually attains its own ends. It is indeed suggestive of the onward march of Rome. Even to-day it would well afford passage for an army.

The scenery of this long drive is not interesting. There are olive orchards so large and so numerous that they become monotonous, and there are almost as many vineyards which are not very picturesque. The peasants do not make such pictures as those about Pau. The piercing power of the mistral forces them to wrap themselves up very closely. Instead of the pretty beretta they wear often a fur cap which is quite commonplace. But there are towers on the hills, very ancient, perhaps Roman, and there are churches here and there, and convents among the olive trees. There are two or three villages, but they have a desolate, forsaken look quite different from most little towns in France. They should not look like this in the midst of such abundant plenty — but they do.

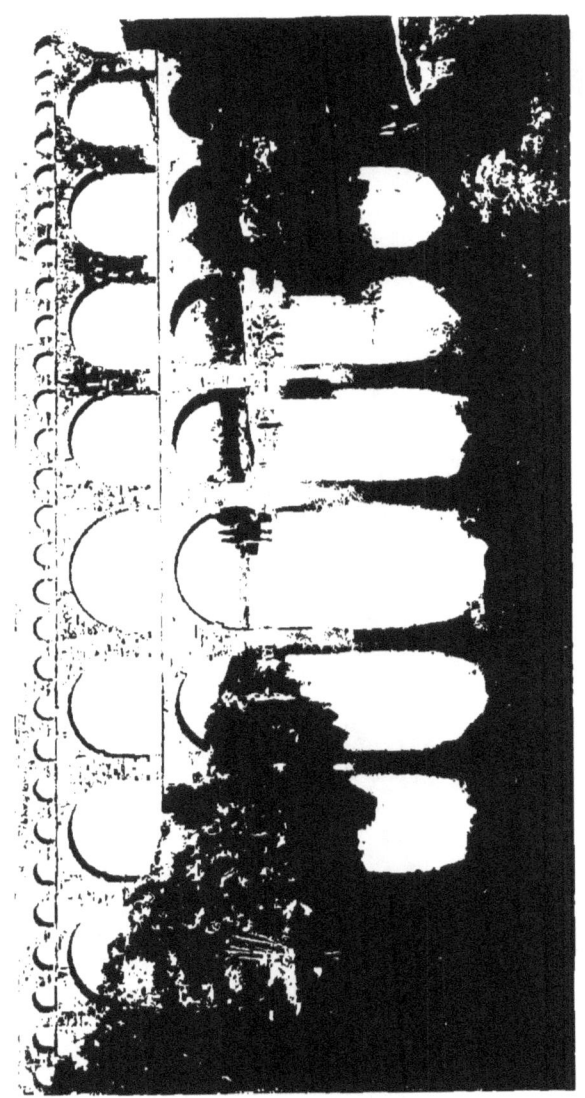

THE PONT DU GARD

On nearing the Pont du Gard the aspect of the country suddenly changes. It is no longer smiling and fertile, but forbidding because of rocks, and cliffs, and wild, lonesome spaces where no habitations are.

Suddenly on turning from the main road and entering a deep gorge through which the river flows, the great bridge is seen. The first sight of it is an impression never to be forgotten. From one mountain to the other, across the stream and the jagged rocks on either side, it stretches. Its towering arches — three tiers of them — seem almost to touch the sky. The first thought about this wonderful structure is of its majesty, the next of its time-defying strength. How many times in all the centuries of its life have the lightning and the wind sought to attack it! How many times have the floods sought to undermine its foundations, and all without avail, for it still stands there. It was built, as it is said, by Marcus Agrippa, the son-in-law of Augustus, nineteen years before Christ was born. Here it stands to-day, almost intact. If man had not touched it, it would be nearly as it was upon the day when it was completed. The elements have had little perceptible effect upon it.

Here is the restless energy of the Roman people, embodied in stone. They wished water for their games at Nemausus, and no physical obstacle was to stand in the way of the accomplishment of their wishes. They cared not for the enormous expense of such a structure. The world was theirs. Why should they care? They thought the world was always to be their world, and therefore they built what was meant to last as long as the very mountains themselves.

But what an extraordinary method of construction for a building that was to last forever! The huge blocks of stone that form these gigantic arches are fitted together without a particle of mortar or cement. They are simply close-joined, and so accurately that there is no space between them anywhere, and they support one another according to the scientific principle of the arch.

How these stones were raised to the dizzy height of one hundred and sixty feet, how they were held in place in the central arch of the second tier whose span is seventy feet, no man understands fully to-day. This arch — one of the grandest and most marvellous in existence — is so broad and so high that the whole Maison Carrée, the Greek temple, could be passed through it without touching anywhere. The arches of the first tier that rise from the rocks by the river are lower and much more massive. Those of the second tier spring upward with a tremendous leap, and in spite of their extreme solidity they produce an effect of almost aerial lightness as they stand out against the sky. The upper arches are much more numerous and a great deal smaller. These directly supported the aqueduct itself. Their effect architecturally is much like that of a cornice, or some other ornamental work crowning the immense structure beneath. Mounting to the top and crossing the bridge through the viaduct there are grand views of the river and the wild gorge, and the construction of the whole bridge becomes more and more wonderful the nearer one approaches it.

The most marvellous view of all is to be had on the river-bank on the other side from that where the bridge is first seen in coming from Nîmes. If the sun is setting it makes this Roman bridge golden, glorious, splendid, as if it were touched by the very spirit of Rome. Yellow arch upon yellow arch rises against the dazzling blue of the sky. Some of them frame in clouds of deep gray or pearly white. Each makes its own picture, and all of them strongly holding hand in hand seem even able to bind the wild mountains together and keep them captive, quite stilled by a power that seems almost as great as their own. It is truly a most suggestive monument to the power of the Imperial city. Strength, majesty, the golden glow in the hour of

sunset — what better can express the spirit of the
Roman Empire?

Arles has been called a Greek city, as contrasted
with Nîmes, which is Roman in its spirit. Nevertheless, there is an amphitheatre here which much resembles that at Nîmes, though it is not so well
preserved. In the Middle Ages this great building
was almost a town in itself. Every arch was made
into a house. It was only necessary to fill up the
opening. The roof was already there. With a low
doorway and a window, the mansion was complete.
Houses were built also within, where the seats formerly were. Some one in the feudal days caught the
idea that such a place must have been meant for a
fortress and therefore four great square towers were
built on the top of the arches of Arles' arena and it
became a mediæval stronghold. In most cities of
these days the houses clung as closely as they could
to the castle, but here there was a more intimate
relation still, for they were a part of the fort itself and
many were within its walls.

The Greek spirit of Arles is more felt in the theatre than anywhere else. This theatre was an immense one. It is said that sixteen thousand people
could be seated in it. Its size suggests rather Rome
than Greece, but the two columns that still remain
of the proscenium are Greek indeed. The whole

row of them, when complete with cornice above, must have been a marvel of beauty. There is much to be studied here, because so many of the details are preserved that it is quite possible to reconstruct in the mind the whole building as it used to be.

Nevertheless, there is nothing else at Arles comparable in beauty for one moment to the cloisters of St. Trophimus. Here are four sides of a cloistered court, and each one represents the art of a century, the eleventh, twelfth, thirteenth, and fourteenth, and there are also Roman and Grecian pillars and pilasters used in the construction of this wonderful place. In some way or other the different styles, the heterogeneous materials, are joined together in such wise that they form one of the most beautiful cloistered courts in the world. There is one more lovely by the church of St. John at Toledo. That at Mont St. Michel is also a most wonderful work of Gothic art, but apart from these two I know of none more exquisite than this. The Romanesque and the Gothic builder seem here to strive together in a generous emulation, each seeking for what is most artistic. The sculptures of the different capitals are most interesting. They are so numerous, so varied, that it would need almost a volume to describe them in detail. The general effect of them is one of an almost incredible richness.

To find the beauty at Arles one must come to these cloisters. The arena and the theatre, impressive, interesting as they are, are not comparable in charm to this work of Christian art, full of thought, inspired by a most devoted, religious spirit, and yet telling of the poetry of this sunny land of Provence.

CHAPTER XXII

BOURGES

In the very old French towns it is natural to expect some picturesqueness of architecture, some quaintness not to be found in modern cities. This is, nevertheless, not the case except in certain places. There are streets, as at Dinan and Blois, where the buildings of the olden time remain, and these streets are most interesting. There are some parts of Bourges also where there are houses with pointed gables and overhanging eaves. These are charming; but apart from them the streets of the town are not of great interest. They ought to be to counteract the effect of the dirt and the bad smells all about, but the city has been largely modernized in its buildings, though not in its drainage.

The principal glory of Bourges is its cathedral. The house of Jacques Cœur, now the Palais de Justice, comes next in interest, and then comes the home of the celebrated lawyer, Cujas, now a museum. These three buildings are quite enough to make any town famous, even if there were nothing else.

The cathedral of Bourges is one of the most peculiar in France, because it has no transepts. It is also one of the most remarkable in the number and variety of its stained glass windows, many of which are very ancient.

The aim of the French Gothic cathedral builders has usually been to produce a profound impression with their façades. At Amiens, at Rouen, at Notre Dame, even at Tours, this effect has been successfully produced, but such is not the case at Bourges. The façade is sadly lacking in harmony. The towers are quite dissimilar in style. The early one at the right is fine twelfth-century Gothic, but it is unfinished, hardly rising above the level of the roof. It is, moreover, marred by a curious building placed against the side of it, the use of which I cannot understand, which forces itself most unpleasantly into the general contour of the façade with which it really has nothing whatever to do. The other tower, called the "butter tower," because built by money paid for indulgences to eat butter in Lent, is much higher, but it is bad in style, with round arches, and florid ornamentation quite out of keeping with true Gothic work. Beside all this the architect wished an immense window at the west end of his church, and therefore he had to use a number of heavy buttresses to support his wall and roof. These break up the

THE CATHEDRAL OF BOURGES

horizontal lines of the façade, and do not substitute any beauty of the perpendicular manner of construction because they are not ornamented, and do not terminate in exquisite pinnacles, gradually diminishing in size, as is the case at Tours.

But after this first disappointment as to the general effect, comes a thrill of wonder and admiration for the details. There are five portals — all most profusely ornamented with sculpture. The richness, delicacy, and expressiveness of this work can hardly be surpassed in the carvings of any cathedral façade in France. The arrangement and the subjects are about the same as at Amiens, Notre Dame, and Tours. There was a tradition about this that came from the Norman days before the Gothic builder began his work. Here, however, there is a charm in the execution so marked as plainly to tell that some really great sculptor did this carving. Nobody knows his name. Nobody knows who built the cathedral — but this is often the case in Gothic buildings. If what the artist did could live, he himself seems to have cared little whether his name would live in fame. There are carvings on the six arches of the central portal of Bourges cathedral worthy of a place even in the cloisters of San Juan de los Reyes at Toledo. Figures of angels and of saints, foliage of vines and trees, cluster about these lofty arches in a way most

fascinating, full of the grace and simplicity of the
highest art.

This central portal is so wonderful that it should
be spoken of more in detail. Each arch has its procession of figures from the top of the supporting
column to the keystone, and each figure has a carved
canopy above it as though it were in a shrine. There
are seventy-six of these figures. The inner arch,
nearest the central figure of the Christ, and the one
next to it are given to the angels, the heavenly choir
who sing the Saviour's praise. Then come the apostles, then the martyrs, each with his palm branch,
and then the saints. On the outermost arch are the
kings of Israel. These had a nobler place in the
façade of Amiens, but even placed as they are here
they are fine and full of expression. The central
subject in the tympanum is the best of all from the
artist's point of view. In the lower panel the dead
are lifting the stones from their graves. The good
arise with folded hands and meek expression. The
wicked are more violent in action, but as works of
sculpture they are more interesting because the anatomy is wonderfully studied considering its very early
date. On one side of the next panel above the good
are being led to Paradise. St. Peter has his arms full
of little children whom he holds in a fold of his robe.
The grown-up good people, with a most self-satisfied

smirk, are walking toward the saint. But here, as below, the action, the real life of the figures is on the side of the wicked, who are being plunged by most extraordinary devils into a cauldron which two imps are heating by blowing the fire beneath it. Between the two groups an angel holds the scales of justice, and with one hand draws to him a little child, a lovely girl, whom a hideous devil is trying to seize. Above, in the upper panel, is the Christ with attendant saints and angels. Though the subject has been so often treated, no sculptor of the early French cathedrals has given to it more expressiveness and finish in detail. The groups in the other four portals and their arches are very remarkable also, but not so well preserved.

These five portals are the glory of the exterior of Bourges cathedral. Apart from them, its impression is that of an immense mass of stone, not harmonious and not beautiful. The buttresses are too numerous and not light enough. They interfere with each other and greatly mar the general effect.

On entering the church, the first impression is of immense length and height. There is nothing to interfere with the vista from one end to the other — not a choir screen, not a break of crossing transepts. The window of the Lady Chapel seems in some dim distance not accurately to be measured in the mind.

The columns rise to a great height; above them is a triforium, above that is the clerestory, above that again is the vaulted roof. So it is from end to end of the great church.

Then comes a feeling of disappointment. The columns of the nave are too high and too thin. Their capitals are too small, and do not project enough. The triforium has not been allowed sufficient space and seems too low, nor is it beautiful in its architecture. The windows far above are beautiful, but they would have been better if they had been brought lower down. Therefore, the lover of architecture, who has come to Bourges, stands in the nave, troubled in his mind, wondering why a church should be so famous that has such glaring faults. If he turns away with such an impression, he makes a great mistake. Let him step into the aisles. There are two of them on each side. Let him go there when the morning sun is illuminating the stained windows.

There are few more inspiring views in all Gothic architecture. The outer aisle is low, but of most magnificent construction, — great piers with clustered columns supporting a vaulted roof quite in harmony with their lines and their strength, and chapels at the side luminous with the light that comes softened through the glass with its infinite variety of color. But there is another aisle more than twice as high as the outer one, — very narrow, very lofty. It stretches away clear to the end of the church and bends around the choir back of the high altar. At the end of it glows a window, red as a ruby. At the end of the outer one is the blue of a sapphire in another window. To stand by the immense columns near the portal and look upon these two aisles at once is like opening some mediæval romance.

This is not all it suggests. The procession of the low aisle to the higher, and thence to the towering nave, seems to lead from the privacy of the chapels that are still without the lower aisle to the full light of the church. From the private prayer and the confessional, the worshipper is led by the very spirit of the building to the great congregation, the high altar, and the mass.

In the aisles is the beauty of Bourges cathedral, and in the stained glass windows, too; for these are no less wonderful than those of Chartres, and even more interesting historically.

The crypt is a most noble structure — one of the finest in Europe. Here are some remarkable monuments, among them an effigy of the Duke de Berri, called the Magnificent, who was nearly related to Charles VII.

There are not many monuments in the church.
There is nothing to tell that Louis XI., who was born
at Bourges, was baptized in this cathedral. That
king whose dungeons are at Loches, whose hangman
lived hard by his castle of Plessis-les-Tours, whose
ability humbled the nobles and made France a kingdom, when he was a little innocent child was brought
into this towering church. The light of its glorious
windows shone upon him, and the priest put the
holy water and the consecrated oil upon his brow,
and signed him with the sign of the cross.

Here, too, Charles VII. came when he was only
"Le Roi de Bourges" before Joan of Arc had
delivered him from the English. Perhaps he even
dared to worship here after his craven spirit had let
her be burnt at the stake without one attempt to
rescue her. Perhaps he even came here to pray
after his dastardly treatment of his noble minister of
finance, Jacques Cœur, who is far more the hero of
Bourges than the king who caused his banishment
and stole his money.

Jacques Cœur built a chapel in the cathedral. It
is now the sacristy. It must have been very beautiful in his day, but now it is filled with woodwork of
a much later date which is neither interesting nor
beautiful.

There is, however, a monument in Bourges to this

famous man, and that is his house. It is called a
house; it must have been a palace. Now it is the
Palais de Justice. The courts are here from the
Justice of the Peace up to the Court of Appeals.
Strange that justice should have come to take up its
abode in the house of one condemned by the courts
with such shameful injustice at the command of the
king, and by the wish of his courtiers.

The house is built partly upon the old Roman
walls, and two of the Roman towers are incorporated
in it. From that side it seems an immense fortified
place and has the cone-topped towers that mark the
early French architecture long before the Renascence. But the other side is the one really characteristic of the building as architects knew it. This
is a most beautiful specimen of early Renascence
architecture, for while it is not harmonious in style
there are exquisite touches in it. The turret at the
left of the portal is a rarely graceful work of this
period. It has the merit of not being too profusely
ornamented, while it has a great deal of the richness
so characteristic of this style.

The portal is even more beautiful. In the projecting balcony above it was once a statue of
Charles VII. It is hardly to be regretted that this
was destroyed at the time of the Revolution. It is
to be deeply regretted, however, that the statue of

P

Jacques Cœur himself, which was in a similar balcony on the inner side of the portal, was destroyed
at the same time. True, there is a white marble
statue of him before the house, but this is a modern
work, and so bad that it is a great pity it should
occupy the place it does. For this man was a great
man. He was a conqueror in the peaceful world of
trade. He was a statesman who managed with con-
summate ability the finances of his country at a time
when that country was almost overwhelmed. He
was a patriot who placed all his wealth at the dis-
posal of his king in the hour of need. Within the
house are many sculptures, which tell of his domestic life. He seems to have been a man who loved
his home, and was devotedly attached to his wife.
Over one chimneypiece in the great hall there are
three panels, each representing the merchant and
his wife playing some game together. In the centre
panel it is chess; the others are not quite so plainly
to be made out.

In the many carvings of this house, other domestic
scenes are represented. Over the kitchen entrance
are figures of servants cleaning pans and preparing
meats for the table. On the central tower of the
court are many figures of those who served the
master of the house in his home and his business;
and there are curious palms and orange and lemon

trees to tell of his traffic with the Orient. Jacques
Cœur must have been something of a soldier, too,
for his motto is, "À vaillants Cœurs rien impossible";
and he must also have been religious, for his coat of
arms consists of a heart and a shell, the latter being
the emblem of a pilgrimage to the shrine of St.
James. Moreover, he built a beautiful chapel in
his home, beside the one at the cathedral. It is said
that a man's house is in a way the expression of his
character; and I think this is emphatically true of
the superb, yet not too richly ornamented, mansion of
the master-merchant of Bourges.

It is true in some degree also of the home of
Cujas, the great lawyer and learned professor. This
is an admirable specimen of early Renascence architecture. The home-feeling has largely left it, because it is now a museum filled with very rare and
curious things, some of them of great interest. The
most interesting are the prie-dieu of the unfortunate
Jeanne de Valois and a death mask of her, and the
portraits of Jacques Cœur and his wife. The whole
second story, which is very large, was devoted to
the library and writing-room of the learned professor; and it is mostly because of the amplitude
of these accommodations that the house can still be
somewhat associated with the life of its occupant.
The raftered ceilings are fine, and so are the chimney·

pieces.　University professors and lawyers must have been well paid in those days, for the whole house is on a scale of great magnificence, though not nearly so extensive as that of the merchant-prince.

The house where Louis XI. was born is a very fine example of the architecture immediately preceding the French Renascence, almost as interesting to an architect as either of the other great houses of Bourges.

The whole impression of the place is emphatically a thought of mediævalism; for it is produced by the overpowering size and glory of the church, the magnificence of the homes where the rich dwelt, and the narrow streets and poor houses where lived those not fortunate enough to be kings, ecclesiastics, merchant-princes, or lawyers.

CHAPTER XXIII

THE CATHEDRAL OF RHEIMS

THE cathedral of Rheims, the church of the French kings, dedicated to the Mother of the King of kings who sits in serene majesty over its portal, seems even among the other great cathedrals the queen of them all. Not even the façade of Amiens is more impressive. There is no façade in all France, perhaps in all the world, so wonderful as this one. Here the Gothic builder has come nearer to a perfect expression of his thought than anywhere else, if the apse of Amiens be excepted. Here is the most perfect beauty of line, the most exquisite ornament, always subservient to the strength of the supporting parts but always aiding their power by the help of its beauty. In no other façade are the towers pierced quite as they are here, for the lancet-windows in them are open to the day. There is no glass there, and through them can be seen the flying buttresses that support the roof of the nave. In Notre Dame, although the towers are pierced in a somewhat similar way, the flying buttresses cannot be seen as here. This effect, unique so far as I know, becomes even more extraordinary when it is remembered that these towers were meant to be carried to nearly twice their present height.

It seems almost impossible that this masonry, which hardly looks like masonry at all because it is so full of sun and air, could be able to support great spires above, but such was the architect's thought. There were to be seven spires of the church of Rheims; now there are none complete as they were originally designed.

The first impression of the façade is so over-powering that it is only possible to admire it, without any attempt to study its details. For a time it is best to let the glorious beauty have its way, and the intense religious spirit of it still the thought and uplift the mind with its own inspiration. Here, as at Amiens, it is best to be silent, seeking no explanation of the parts that together join in forming this beautiful whole, but hoping that the spell of its almost inexplicable charm, its deeply religious spirit, will remain in the mind and in the heart always.

After a while it is necessary to study more closely this façade of the kings and the queens, that it may be known how this great thing has been done. All the meanings of it cannot be understood without

THE CATHEDRAL OF RHEIMS

study, but most of them are not very difficult to comprehend. The position of the kings at the highest part of the façade until the towers begin to rise from it is very significant. At Amiens their position was lofty enough, but here it is far nearer the sky line. The builder must have meant to suggest that the kings were indeed the divinely anointed, called by the Lord to rule over the people.

The figures of these monarchs are so majestic in their expression, so grandly conceived, so imposing in form, so perfectly placed in their towering niches crowned by pinnacles most richly ornamented, that they do succeed in bringing to the mind an almost irresistible conviction that kings are nearer heaven than other people.

This is not the most inspiring thought a church could give, but it was well to suggest it here over the entrance to the place of the coronation of the kings of France. By so doing, it is quite possible the architect meant to teach a lesson, unfortunately not always learned by kings,—the lesson of their responsibility to a higher ruler.

For this reason, doubtless, the stories of David and of Solomon are told in the sculptures below, and many other stories are there told which might help these exalted people to know and to do their duties to their kingdom. In some of these sculptures there is a spirit that strongly recalls Michael Angelo's David, the stripling about to be a king, not knowing it, but full of faith in the one King.

The beauty and the meaning of the exterior of Rheims cathedral are by no means confined to the façade. There is a procession of saints and angels that goes on all about the church like the frescoes of Flandrin in St. Germain des Prés. There are many angels with outstretched wings in the pinnacled shrines that seem like chapels uplifted toward the sky, who have not gone far away from the kings — only far enough to guard the church in which they are to be crowned. They surround it on every side. They brood over it. They wish to protect it and to help those who are here consecrated to the task of influencing and directing the life of a great people. These angels are a triumph of Gothic art. The suggestion they give is poetic and religious. The long succession of pinnacled shrines in which they stand is ornamental in the highest degree, and helps more than anything else about it to make the side view of Rheims one of the most beautiful in the world.

Not only are the kings thus uplifted and protected, but they are also taught their duty as Christians. The most prominent place in all the sculptural work of the façade is given to the baptism of Clovis. The king is in the baptismal font—half immersed there.

He is in the very centre of the upper part of the façade, and directly above him rises its highest and most richly ornamented pinnacle. There is nothing in the church higher than that except the towers.

It is St. Remy who baptizes the king. There are other saints about him. St. Thierry holds the archbishop's cross. A king who had preceded Clovis holds the sceptre. St. Montan has in his hands the royal mantle. The scales of justice are held up by another king, who shows them to the monarch who is just entering upon his work as a Christian ruler. Below are the soldiers in armor, who were baptized with their king.

This subject was thought to be so important that not only does it hold the most prominent place on the façade, but it is also repeated in smaller figures and a different arrangement over the portal of the north entrance.

Beneath this portal is a figure of the Saviour, wonderful in dignity and spirituality, a veritable masterpiece of the sculpture of those early days. It should have a more prominent place than is generally given to it in describing the sculptures of this exterior. The reason is that the portal at the side has no such prominence as that of the façade, where the Madonna sits enthroned because it is her church. As a work of sculpture the figure of the Saviour is far finer than that of the Virgin Mary. It has more of the modern spirit, the delicacy of touch, the intellectual quality, that were not fully developed until much later in French art.

All that I have said thus far has to do with the exterior, nor does it nearly even suggest what ought to be said of that part of this royal and religiously inspired building.

Within are glories harder to tell about than those without. The nave is one of the most perfect ever built by a Gothic architect. The columns, the arches they support, the triforium, the clerestory, are in such perfect relation of form, proportion, and color that they seem like a realized dream. But even such forms and colors as these are not the chief beauty of this interior.

Far behind the high altar is a place whence can be seen the windows toward the west. In no other church that I know has such an effect been produced. The western wall seems all glass, held in place in some mysterious way not to be understood within the church. It is not meant that the supporting part should be seen from this side. The thought of the builder was that this western wall of his church, should be not a wall but the most magnificent glory of color that could possibly be attained. This has to do with the royal spirit of the church, for it seems one vast collection of gems. The ruby and the emerald are most prominent, but the sapphire and the topaz have their place also. There is no re-production possible either in words or pictures of such a thing as this. Even in looking at it one wonders if it can be really there.

The best place from which to see it is almost the very spot where stood Charles VII. to receive his crown, while Joan of Arc stood beside him. This maiden of France had truly a right to be in this church whose porch the Virgin guards, whose tran-sept is sculptured without with the story of that Virgin's assumption. The triumph of Joan of Arc hardly seems to be one that young girls would naturally seek, but it was the Virgin whom she saw in her visions at Domrémy. Now her work is done, and there is again a kingdom of France. When the crown of the land she loved had been placed on the king's head, it seemed to her that it would be better now to go back again to her sheep and her orchard at the old home where she had seen the visions which had meant so much to France. It was a most touching thought of truest humility, but the life of this inspired girl was to have its tragic end, and the peaceful peasant home was not to shelter her more.

Many another king has been crowned here since

that day. The splendor attendant on such ceremonies is attested by the richness of the robes in the
sacristy, and the magnificence of the gifts given by
the kings at the time of their coronation. Some of
these gifts are very curious. There are relics, one
of which seems a singularly appropriate present from
a king of France, whose crown was not always easy
on his head, for it is a thorn of the Saviour's crown
of thorns. One of the kings gave a most curious
representation of St. Ursula and her virgins in their
ship. This is made almost entirely of silver.

Henry II. gave a most remarkable little group of
figures, the subject of which is the scene of the
resurrection. The Saviour sits upon the edge of
the tomb. His figure is of silver. The Roman
soldier sleeps in front of the opened sepulchre. This
is a beautifully modelled gold figure attributed to
Benvenuto Cellini. This king had the almost
incredible irreverence to ornament this work in .
places with the crescent, the emblem of Diane de
Poitiers. He did the same thing in the chapel at
Fontainebleau. His human and spiritual loves seem
to have been most strangely mixed together.

Many of the treasures here were destroyed at the
time of the Revolution, but enough remain to show
what the custom of the French kings was at the time
of their coronation. They gave superb robes to be

worn by the prelate who crowned them, and costly vessels for the service of the altar. The chasuble used by the prelate who crowned Louis XIV. is of silver and gold, ornamented by six pearls of purest lustre, each one of them nearly as large as the egg of a robin. The treasures given by Charles X. — the last king crowned here — are more numerous than any others now remaining in the sacristy. They are splendid, almost all of gold, but in artistic workmanship they do not equal those of the earlier centuries.

When the kings came to Rheims to be crowned they dwelt in the palace of the archbishop, close beside the church. In that palace is a grand hall where the coronation banquet took place. There are reception rooms, and sleeping-rooms, salons, and a salle des gardes for the soldiers who have always been needed about the person of a French monarch. There is a chapel where high mass was celebrated by the prelate for his royal guest. In this chapel now stands a statue of Urban II., the French Pope, who is represented in the act of proclaiming the first crusade. This statue was not here when Philip Augustus was crowned. Perhaps he would not have deserted Richard Cœur de Lion if he had learned its lesson of enthusiasm and faith stronger than life itself. The statue is not a masterpiece of sculpture, but it has in it a most marvellous spirit of religious fervor.

In these halls — in this chapel — were the kings. Joan of Arc did not stay here. She was the real arbiter of her country's destinies then; but royal apartments were not for her.

Now there are no more kings crowned at Rheims. It may be that there never will be any more. The people have the power they wished for. May it be hoped that in this royal church they will seek a blessing on that power, and that it may be granted to them!

If they come flocking thither in the evening hour just as the sun is setting, they will find the façade transformed, filled through and through with the glory of the kings and the saints who have passed away. It is golden — almost like the ruddy gold of Rome that belongs with the diadems of kings. Each statue wakes to life. The coldness of the old stone is gone. The sunshine of the glorious days of French history has banished it. The light of religion in which dwell the saints and the angels is upon it. The tender spirit of the Mother is there and the uplifting power of the Christ is in it. In such a light as this the façade of Rheims cathedral must have given a benediction and an inspiration to the kings who entered this golden portal to receive their crowns before the altar.

CHAPTER XXIV

To Rheims the kings came for their coronation; at St. Denis their bodies were laid to rest. In the one church is the splendor surrounding a king whose reign has just begun with high hope that it may be well for his people and himself while he holds the sceptre. In the other church is the sadness that comes with the end of human life, the regret that even consecrated kings fail often in doing their simple duty.

St. Denis is a very old church. The first building was a basilica erected by Christians as soon as they were allowed to build churches in France. It was built to commemorate the martyrdom of St. Denis and his companions, — the priest Rustique and the deacon Eleuthère. Afterward St. Geneviève caused it to be rebuilt about the end of the fifth century. Dagobert I., in fulfilment of a vow to the holy martyrs, built a still greater church upon the same site. This lasted a century and a half, and then King

Pepin commenced a new church, which Charlemagne finished.

This church was destroyed by the Normans. King after king has restored or rebuilt this abbey of the first Archbishop of Paris.

At last it became a temple of Reason in the time of the Revolution, but even that did not prevent its destruction. A restoration was begun about the beginning of this century, but it was M. Viollet-le-Duc who finally made the church what it now is. This great architect has shown here the same skill and patience that have brought to life again so many of the ruined monuments of France.

The façade of the church is very peculiar. It is partly Norman, partly Gothic; but the strangest thing about it is the battlement that surmounts it. This strongly suggests the fortress idea, and recalls the Church of the Templars at Luz. There are, however, no traces of exterior walls about St. Denis. It is possible the monks were here at one time, as good soldiers as their brethren of St. Michel. Doubtless, they had the same need of carnal weapons to defend their sacred places.

The interior of the church is very beautiful, but not as impressive as any of the other cathedrals, because it is so new. The softening touch of age is not upon its columns and arches nor upon its stained glass windows.

ST. DENIS

Admirable as the restoration is, it cannot conceal the fact that the nave and the choir, the chapels and the vaulted roof, are not those which in the olden time sheltered the remains of the French kings.

It is strange to think of the great antiquity of this building; to remember that Clovis, and Dagobert, and Charlemagne are associated with it; that most of the great kings of France have been buried here; and that, nevertheless, it was restored, brought to life again at a time when there were no more kings to be buried in this place of the dead monarchs. With all the pains they took to raise this splendid mausoleum, when the Revolution came their ashes were scattered to the winds. Nothing is left of the power they had on earth except as the impress of it may have touched the life of the French people and made it better or worse.

The monuments are here, — not all as they were, for many have been destroyed; but some are preserved, and these make the chief interest of the church. Those that remain were replaced by M. Viollet-Le-Duc, as nearly as possible in the positions they formerly occupied. Their tale of the end of earthly power is what is told at St. Denis.

Let the monuments speak for themselves. Here is Clovis I., whose baptism is told of on the façade of Rheims. The sculpture is rude, but there is a

Q

certain majesty about it, especially in the way the sceptre is held, the commanding gesture of the left hand, and the crouching lion beneath the feet. The leading figure of the kings at Rheims now lies prostrate in this church of the dead. He has many companions in his last sleep. King after king, queen after queen, surround him. Dagobert has his chapel here, and there is many a bas-relief to tell the wonderful story of how his soul was saved from the devils by St. Denis, St. Maurice, and St. Martin.

There are many kings below in the Norman crypt, whose massive columns strongly suggest the power of that kingdom whose king was once a Charlemagne.

In the inner part of the crypt are many sarcophagi, in which were the bodies of the Bourbons. How many ages of the world's history are suggested in this church! It is almost as if every century of Christian times had some royal person here to tell its tale.

Beside the kings, there are knights and soldiers. Du Guesclin, the most valiant defender of France against the English, has a monument here. The effigy of this brave man is, unfortunately, but a very poor thing. It surely cannot give any idea of his bodily power, for he seems like a boy in height, nor is there any indication of such muscular strength as must have been needed to resist the sturdy English knights of those days. But the spirit of the

French champion is here, and it is well that it dwells so near the kings in their last resting-place.

It is a pity that Joan of Arc is not here. The French kings needed many to help them, though some were well able to take care of themselves. Louis XII. and Francis I. fought their own battles, and fought them bravely, although at Pavia Francis was defeated and captured.

The monuments to these two kings and their wives are among the most remarkable that any kings or queens have ever had made in their honor. The same idea is carried out in both, and they were evidently the work of very able sculptors, who had agreed together about how a monument to kings should be constructed.

It is astonishing that any great artist should ever have dreamed of doing what has been done here. The principle on which the sculptor carried out his design seems to have been a contrast, as strong as he could possibly make it, between life and death. He puts life above and death beneath.

Francis I. and his queen, Claude de France, are kneeling together upon what might be called the roof of the tomb. They are clad in royal robes. All the splendor of their insignia is about them. Their prie-dieus are richly ornamented. It is the

same with Louis XII. and Anne of Brittany, with
Henry II. and Catherine de' Medici.

Below are figures nearly naked, which seek to
express the very death-agony itself. That of Francis,
attributed by some to Jean Goujon, by others to
Pierre Bontemps, is a masterpiece in the study of
anatomy. The king's head has fallen back over his
pillow. He is breathing his last gasp. Every muscle
is tense with the strain of the final struggle. The
last peace does not seem to be there, even although
the body has yielded to death. It is almost as if one
heard the latest breath of the king and was there .
when his death struggle came.

But why should the figure be nude? Why should
the figure of the dead queen be nude? It seems as
if the sculptor had chosen to bring the body, almost at
the moment of death, close to the sepulchre that was
to receive it. The sepulchre was below. On the
tomb of Louis XII. and Anne of Brittany it is surrounded by the twelve apostles, exquisitely carved in
marble. But above the artist seems to have thought
it best to tell a tale of kingly grandeur, and to use in
telling it all the outward splendors that surround a
king.

I have never seen such light and shade as this.
It suggests Rembrandt's "Lesson in Anatomy," but
even there the contrast is not nearly so strong; for

the dead man and the living doctors had no such relation together as the dead kings and queens and their full-robed selves above. There is much beauty in the ornament of these tombs.

After the artist had finished his ghastly portraits of the dead, human body, even kings of men stripped of everything but that, after he had shown how great and glorious were these royal people in their life, he calls upon religion and poetry to ornament their resting-places, to give them thoughts of a life to come, as well as those of the life that was ended.

Some of the bas-reliefs about these monuments are exquisite in design. They tell of battles for the most part, for here is the history of the kings written in marble, but the surrounding figures seem almost like the protecting angels of the cathedral of Rheims. It is strange to see Catherine de' Medici here in prayer, apparently most devout, when those whom she is supposed to have poisoned are lying all about her. It is stranger yet that her nude figure, lying beside that of her husband, should be represented in sleep — not in death. This queen did not like the thought of death. She preferred sleep and forgetfulness. I wonder if she herself ever gave that idea to the sculptor. It is certain that she is so represented here, and some one must have told the artist to make this surprising change, a contrast between sleep and death.

The statues of Anne of Brittany, both in life and death, do not suggest the active, ambitious character of the Breton queen. They are too demure in expression, but it may be well to give a thought of peace about a life that was almost always troubled.

Henry II. could not bring Diane de Poitiers here. In many a church and palace he had associated her with him, but in this church of the dead he has no companion but the queen who feared to die.

This is true of Francis also, and of many another.

Here they came at last. Here the pleasures and luxuries of life are forgotten, and the duties of a king and a queen are remembered.

The lesson of the façade of Rheims, the inspiration of the kings about to be crowned, is enforced by sombre St. Denis, where all these royal people once lay dead, called away from their earthly glory to make answer to the use they made of the high place they had been called upon to fill.

CHAPTER XXV

ST. ETIENNE DU MONT, THE CHURCH OF THE PATRON SAINT OF PARIS — NOTRE DAME, AND THE PANTHÉON

AT St. Denis it seemed as if all ended with death. The gloom of that burial-place is like a heavy pall over a bier. Nevertheless, those who have done well are not forgotten. They live in the memory of a grateful people. The saints who gave their lives to bring the truth of Christ to France; the heroes who gave their lives also to protect their land against a foe; the kings and queens who ruled well, made good laws, founded great institutions of learning, and cared for the poor and the helpless, — all these are still a part of French life. They are not dead, but live in the hearts of the people. Those people, grateful for their good works, have called upon their artists to commemorate them.

Nobly and well has this tribute of gratitude been paid. Great churches have been built in their honor, great paintings tell of their good deeds, great statues keep them living in the midst of the people they loved and died for.

Over the portal of St. Etienne du Mont, the church of the patron saint of Paris, is the stoning of the first martyr, Stephen. Within the church is the tomb of St. Geneviève, who healed and blessed the sick and the poor. So beneficent was her life that this peasant girl of Nanterre was chosen to be the most revered of all the saints by the people of Paris.

The church that was built in her honor is no longer as it used to be. It has been replaced by a larger one, but the building that now stands here is one of the most interesting of the French churches.

This place where St. Geneviève is buried is close beside the Panthéon, the hall of the French heroes. Once the tomb of the saint was on the very spot where it now stands. Once the Panthéon itself was dedicated to her during the short time while the present building was a place of worship. On the other side of the street of King Clovis that passes by it, is still a tower that was a part of the Abbey of St. Geneviève.

The saints and the heroes are brought closely together here. In the Panthéon are the tales of all their deeds as painters alone can tell them. The frescoes of Puvis de Chavanne tell of St. Geneviève

THE CHURCH OF ST. ÉTIENNE DU MONT

in her country home and afterward of her meeting
with the good priests who have been to England to
combat heresy.   In Laurens' work the death of the
saint is vividly portrayed.

Not only are the saints told of here; the great
deeds of the heroes are also vividly protrayed.   There
is the coronation of Charlemagne.   The Pope is
placing the crown on his head.   The church gives
its benediction upon the work which the conquering emperor had done.   What a work it was!
Long years have passed and still its power is felt.

St. Louis sits here in the Panthéon giving justice
to all.   He founds the Sorbonne.   His intense religious ardor calls him to undertake a last crusade.
He meets the Moor.   He is overcome, but not by
force of arms.   The deadly fever conquered him at
last.   Here in the Panthéon he still stands at the
door of his tent, pale but dauntless, meeting those
who came to treat with him for peace.   In a little
time he will go back into that tent and give up his
earthly life; a life that he had tried to use for the
best that he knew,—the advancement of his people
in religion and knowledge.

St. Denis is here.   Bonnat has well told the story
of his martyrdom.   His beheaded companions lie on
the steps of the building where their execution took
place.   He has a halo of glory about the neck, from

which the head has just been stricken. Stooping
down he takes up the head again, and about that
too is a radiance, — the shining light of a life well
lived.

Joan of Arc is here again. In all French life her
spirit lives. Her vision of Domrémy is seen. The
stern battle at Orleans is portrayed. The fearless
girl stands holding her holy banner while the soldiers storm the gate. Afterward, all clothed in
white, she stands upon the fagots which the soldiers
are lighting with their torches. The priest is there.
He has himself mounted upon the fagots and come
as close as he could to the maiden who is bound to
the stake. He holds high a crucifix. It is close to
her lips. He blesses her and prays. Below, but
close also to the fagots, is another priest, who chants
the prayers for those about to die. The English
priests and soldiers are in the background, awaiting
the consummation of this fearful tragedy. It was
ended at last. The flames destroyed the mortal part
of that maiden who made France a kingdom by
repelling the invader and invoking the spirit of
patriotism with the blessing of religion upon it.

Other saints, other kings, are here in this hall of
the heroes, — many of them, — but there is no one who
did so much for France as did the maid of Domrémy;
no king who helped more to bring about good things

for his people than the sainted Louis who died in his crusade for his faith's sake.

Without these two there might have been no Notre Dame, the grand cathedral in the very midst of the greatest of French cities. Here it stands to-day, with the river flowing about it. Here rise its towers toward the sky. Upon its façade are told the stories of what is best in life, what saddest in death.

Within are great columns, magnificent vaulted aisles. There are tombs of martyrs, not only those of olden time, but of to-day also; for here is the monument to the archbishop who was killed at the time of the Commune, and here, also, are the tombs of many priests and others who in these latter days have helped to bring the truth of Christ to the people.

Above are the windows — the glorious windows, full of color, suggestive of all the splendor of a great people, suggestive also of the city that is to be hereafter when the heavens are opened and all see the place that has been prepared above.

This great cathedral! How wonderful it is! Its buttresses are time-defying. Its towers reach toward the sky. This is the home of the religion of France. Here is what her heroes have fought for. Here is what her saints have given their lives for.

The people come into these grand aisles, and sit

beneath a light of story and of glory that shines upon them from the vast windows. They worship in the church that the heroic deeds of others have given to them. It would be well to walk quietly about the aisles, to stop at each chapel, to look on each window, to feel the power of every grand column, the uplifting spirit of every Gothic arch, and then remember that self-sacrifice has made it possible that France should have such monuments as these.

Norwood Press :
J. S. Cushing & Co. — Berwick & Smith.
Norwood, Mass., U.S.A.